G000111635

PASS LEVEL 2

WJEC
Functional Skills English
Pass Level 2

Michael Ross Stuart Sage Natalie Simpson Consultant: Don Astley

www.pearsonschoolsandfecolleges.co.uk

✓ Free online support
✓ Useful weblinks
✓ 24 hour online ordering

0845 630 33 33

Heinemann

Part of Pearson

Contents

Introduction

How does this book work?

This book is designed to help students achieve Level 2 in the WJEC Functional Skills English qualification, and is tailored to the requirements of the specification. It is divided into Reading, Speaking, listening and communication, and Writing sections, with additional material on understanding and tackling the assessments. Each section includes:

▶ an introduction to how students will be assessed

▶ teaching and learning pages addressing the assessment criteria (standards)

▶ practice examination-style tasks and sample answers at Level 2 Fail and Pass, with examiner commentary

▶ self/peer assessment guidance built in throughout to encourage students to appraise and improve their skills.

The units of work are loosely linked around the themes of healthy living, school, teenagers' rights and the community, to enable meaningful links to be made across lessons.

Teacher Guide

Additional support is offered in the Teacher Guide, with practical lesson plans and a wealth of assessment practice and guidance.

About the authors

The authors of both books have been classroom teachers and examiners, and for many years have run workshops and training sessions with teachers. They have been involved with the development of Functional Skills from its inception, and their work has included the setting and assessing of Functional Skills English papers. They have drawn on their wide and varied experience to produce materials that are interesting, informative and instructional. The books can be used with confidence to help students to develop and achieve the best results they can in their Functional Skills English assessments and go on to be confident readers, writers and communicators in all aspects of their lives.

Michael Ross

Natalie Simpson

Stuart Sage

Don Astley

Reading

Introduction

As part of your Functional Skills English assessment you will be tested on your reading skills, using the kinds of texts that are used in everyday life. You must be able to identify what a text is for, what the writer's viewpoint is, how effective the text is, and consider what readers might do after reading the text. For example, you might be asked to read newspaper articles, web pages, advertisements, leaflets or instruction manuals, perhaps including graphs, charts, tables and pictures. You will be asked to use the information you have read to answer questions.

How to use the Reading section of this book

Each double page spread focuses on a different reading skill that you will need to use in the examination. Through texts, teaching and activities, you will learn and practise each essential reading skill. Read the learning objectives carefully to be clear what your aims are, and use the examiner tips for hints on how to pass Level 2. Use them to assess your learning to help you work towards Level 2.

At the end of the section, you will find a sample Reading test to help you practise using your reading skills. There are also two sample student answers, with comments from the examiner, to help you work out what you have done well and what you need to improve on in your own work. For more information on how you will be assessed, see pages 103–11.

ACTIVITY

1 Discuss the assessment criteria.
2 Produce a list of bullet points called 'To pass Level 2 I need to…'. List the most important points you will need to remember in your Reading assessment.
3 Decide which areas you are weakest in, and make sure you focus on improving your skills in these areas.

Assessment criteria

The table below lists and explains the criteria against which your reading will be assessed. It directs you to the pages in this book that teach and practise each skill.

Select, read, understand and compare texts, and use them to gather information, ideas, arguments and opinions.		
Select and use different types of texts to obtain and utilise relevant information	This means using a range of texts and reading skills to find information, and explain what you have found out. By doing this you will get used to different styles used by writers and how they get across their points or information. In a Reading assessment, you need to identify key words in the question. Only write down information that you are asked for.	See pages 6/7, 8/9, 10/11
Read and summarise, succinctly, information/ideas from different sources	This means presenting information from a text clearly but in fewer words. You need to read two or more texts and summarise information from them.	See pages 12/13, 14/15, 16/17
Identify the purposes of texts and comment on how meaning is conveyed	This means working out the text's purpose – what the writer is trying to achieve – and deciding how effective the writing is. Remember, a text can have more than one purpose. You may be asked to consider the use of facts and opinions.	See pages 18/19, 20/21, 22/23
Detect point of view, implicit meaning and/or bias	This means working out what the writer thinks or believes. This may be clearly stated, or it may be suggested in the language they use. You may have to work like a detective, picking up clues in the text. You may need to look for bias.	See pages 24/25, 26/27
Analyse texts in relation to audience needs and consider suitable responses	This means reading a text in detail, and considering what actions its audience might take in response to it. For example, you might be asked to reply to a letter, or present some of the information in a new text. You must make sure your answer is based only on the texts you have read.	See pages 28/29, 30/31
All Reading standards	Practice Reading tasks and sample student answers.	See pages 32–39

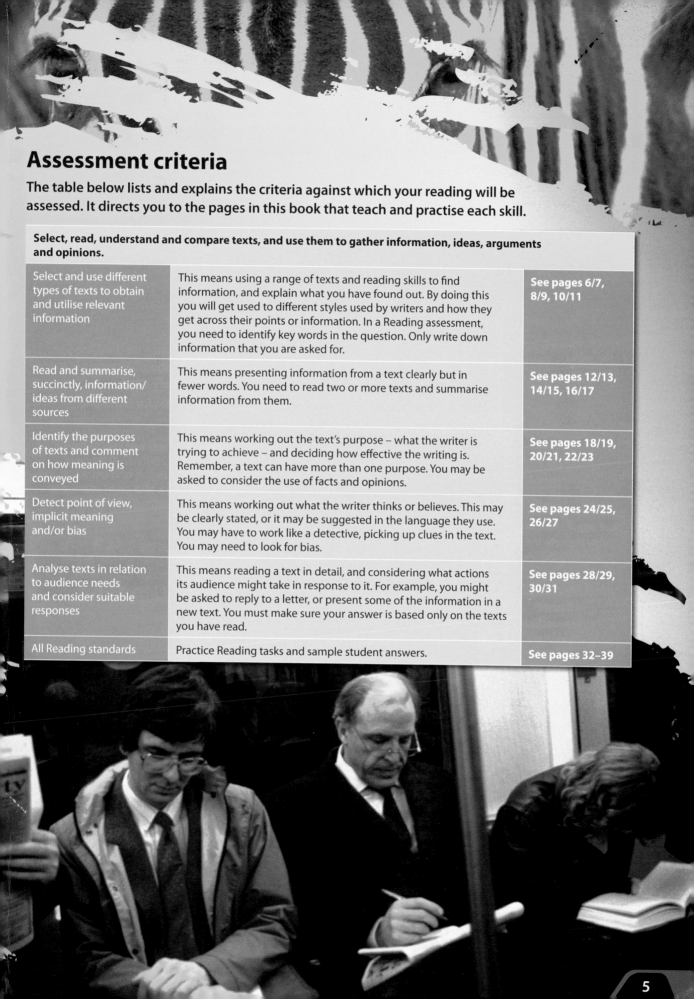

My learning objectives ▼

- To be clear about what information examination questions are asking for
- To read different texts to find and use information
- To practise skimming texts for information

Skimming

TASK: To learn and practise a range of reading skills in obtaining relevant information from texts in order to answer Functional Skills English examination-style questions.

Skimming strategies

To get a general idea of what a text is about so that you can locate information, you can use a technique called skimming. This means focusing on different parts of a text to search for the main idea and particular information. Skimming is much quicker than ordinary reading because you do not read every word.

Look at the text below. The annotations give some strategies for skimming.

Peer/Self-assessment

Look at the learning objectives. Think about what you can do confidently, and what you still need to learn or practise to achieve Level 2.

Read the title first to help you understand the main idea of the text.

Look at any illustrations. They may indicate the main focus or relevant information.

Read any sections in bold. They may include something important.

Look at organisational features such as numbered lists or subheadings. These are often used to show a change in topic, and can help you find information quickly.

Read the first sentence of every section or paragraph to help you understand the topic of each paragraph so you can locate information quickly.

WHAT DRUGS DO TO YOU

Almost half of 16- to 24-year-olds in England and Wales have tried illegal drugs. But the five most commonly taken substances all pose serious dangers.

Illegal drugs are responsible for between 1,300 and 1,400 deaths a year in Britain. They also wreck thousands of relationships, families, and careers.

According to the 2007/08 British Crime Survey, the five most commonly used drugs in Britain are:

1. Cannabis
7.4% of 16- to 59-year-olds reported using cannabis in the previous year. There's evidence of a link between cannabis and mental health problems, such as schizophrenia. Research has shown that smoking cannabis joints is even more damaging to lungs than smoking cigarettes. Long-term use can cause lung disease and cancer. Cannabis use can also cause lack of motivation and paranoia.

2. Cocaine
2.3% of respondents admitted to having taken cocaine in 2006/07. Cocaine is highly addictive. People who are young and healthy can have a fit or heart attack after taking too much coke. It can also cause panic attacks.

3. Ecstasy
The study revealed that 1.5% of 16- to 59-year-olds had taken ecstasy in the previous year, although its use is decreasing. Ecstasy can cause panic attacks or psychotic states. There have been over 200 ecstasy-related deaths in the UK since 1996 and ecstasy has been linked to liver, kidney and heart problems.

4. Hallucinogens
1.4% of participants had used hallucinogens (including LSD and magic mushrooms), which are Class A drugs. Even possession can get you up to seven years in jail. The side-effects, which are random and occasionally very frightening, may include flashbacks.

5. Amphetamines
Amphetamine use was recorded among 1.0% of 16- to 59-year-olds. Amphetamines, also known as 'speed', are very addictive and the comedown can make you feel lousy and depressed. They put a strain on your heart and users have died from overdosing.

Skim through the whole text looking for any key words. In an exam, that often means words that have been used in the question.

ACTIVITY 1

Practise using the strategies in the annotations to skim the text on page 6 for answers to these questions.

1 What is the main idea of the text?
2 List the drugs covered in the article.
3 What proportion of 16- to 24-year-olds have tried illegal drugs?

Before you start to skim a text in the examination, you need to read the question closely to be sure of exactly what you are looking for. To do this, you should identify the key words in the question.

ACTIVITY 2

1 Look at the question below. Read the annotations to find out *exactly* what the examiner is looking for.

'List' means that you are looking for simple facts. You do not need any explanation in this answer.

Key words are 'health problems'. Skim for these, and ignore other information, such as numbers of those using drugs.

List five health problems associated with illegal drugs.

In this question, you are told to find five points. In other questions, look out for whether the word is plural to tell you if you need to find more than one example.

In this case, the whole article is about drugs, but where a text covers several topics, make sure you only search for the topic you are asked about.

2 Now identify the key words in the question below. Write a sentence to sum up what information the question is asking you to find out.

List the ways in which cannabis may affect your health.

When you are in an examination, stop and think of the strategies you can use in reading to find information quickly. Then use them!

ACTIVITY 3

Skim the text below. Pick out the key words while you are reading. Write down in no more than ten words what you think the passage is about.

THE CANNABIS EFFECT

Cannabis is the main drug of concern when it comes to driving. It is known to impair co-ordination and vision. The fact that cannabis can be found in blood up to six weeks after last use demonstrates how difficult it is to know whether or not a driver's ability has been affected by using the drug. Although cannabis is easily detectable with a simple test, it is difficult to prove exactly when someone took it or whether it impaired their driving performance at the time of an accident.

My learning objectives ▼
- To be clear about what information examination questions are asking for
- To read different texts to find and use information
- To practise scanning texts for information

Scanning

TASK: Remind yourself of the task on page 6 before working through these pages.

Scanning strategies

Scanning is a speed-reading skill for locating information quickly. It involves moving your eyes quickly down a page looking for specific information or key words. Once you have scanned a document you might go on to skim it for additional information. Scanning is often used to look for information in a book index or contents list. You might scan the website options listed by a search engine, looking for the key words that are relevant to your search.

You might find it useful to scan for:

- **key words** – they might be in bold, a different colour or underlined
- **signpost words** – these are words like 'next', 'secondly', 'additionally' that may indicate a change of topic or theme
- **numbers** – if the question asks about a number or quantity, you can scan for that number.

As well as key words, look out for these words that are often used in questions.

What: you should look for information. Check how many marks the question is worth – this will indicate how many points you need to find.

List: you should look for several pieces of information and present them as a list.

Find: you should look for information – the question should tell you how to present it, and the number of marks will tell you how much to look for.

Where: you should look for words relating to place.

When: you should look for words relating to time.

ACTIVITY

1 Read the questions below. The examiner has added notes of what you need to scan for. Use the notes to practise scanning the article opposite for the answers to the questions.

> The keyword is serve – scan the article looking for this word to find the answer.

> 'When' means you could look for a number giving time. Or you can look for the other key words: bread and toaster.

  a How should you serve a boiled egg, according to the article?
  b When should you put your bread in the toaster?
  c How many adults were asked questions in the survey by Veetee Dine?

> 'How many' means you could scan for a number giving a quantity – then read the sentence around the number to make sure it is relevant. Or scan the text looking for the key words 'adults', 'survey' or 'Veetee Dine'.

2 Read the following questions. What key numbers and words used in the questions might you scan for to help you find the required information quickly?

  a How long do two-thirds of young adults spend in the kitchen each evening?
  b What percentage of people claimed they cannot get it right when cooking rice?
  c How many of the people questioned tuck into ready meals at least twice a week?
  d If you want a really hard boiled egg, how long should you leave it in boiling water?

3 Scan the article for your chosen key words to find answers to the questions.

4 Discuss the activity – did you choose the right key words? Would different key words have helped you to find the answers more quickly or accurately?

Britain: The nation that can't even boil an egg

By **Jo Willey**

Britain may be a nation of food lovers but when it comes to cooking up a meal, it seems we've failed to crack it.

The nation's culinary skills have sunk to such a low that 35 per cent of adults admit they cannot even boil an egg.

As an obesity epidemic grips the country, a study has found that the ready meal and microwave have turned us into a nation of three-minute chefs.

Half of those questioned confessed that they tuck into a ready meal at least twice a week.

And it is not a lack of time they cite as the main factor for failing to get out the pots and pans; they said it was a lack of culinary skills that defeated them.

The survey of 2,000 adults, carried out by rice firm Veetee Dine, found that despite watching the TV shows of chefs such as Gordon Ramsay and Jamie Oliver, few people are inspired to try the recipes at home.

This is made clear by the fact that 68 per cent said they cannot get it right when cooking rice. They either leave it in the pan for too long or not long enough.

Runny

Perhaps even more surprising is that 35 per cent also admit they get it wrong when boiling an egg, ending up with something too runny or too hard.

Nearly half of men – 47 per cent – are so inhibited by their lack of ability that they will pass off a ready meal as homemade when trying to impress a woman.

And 71 per cent rely increasingly on microwaves, compared with 20 per cent of previous generations who used the machines.

Two-thirds of young adults spend less than half an hour in the kitchen each evening compared with the hour spent by their parents' generation.

And the availability and increasing quality of quick-to-cook products suggests the situation is unlikely to get any better.

Chef Antony Worrall Thompson, a *Daily Express* columnist, blamed the lack of cookery classes in schools for the trend.

He said, 'It is not surprising when the government has allowed cooking in schools to disappear off the curriculum. Every person needs to know the basics of how to cook.

'I feel in despair. It is important we learn to cook because we are going to get worse and worse health-wise if we don't.'

Simple steps to get it right every time

If you're one of the thousands of adults struggling to make the perfect boiled egg, help is at hand.

Here is *Daily Express* columnist and celebrity chef Antony Worrall Thompson's guide to ensuring success every time:

- Put water in a pan and bring to the boil.
- **Have eggs at room temperature – this will help stop them cracking in the boiling water.**
- Pop the eggs into the water and set the timer for four minutes. The timing is for a medium-sized egg.
- **Put bread in the toaster at the same time.**
- After four minutes take the egg from the water and chop off the top.
- **Serve with buttered soldiers.**
- The egg should have a mostly hard white with a runny yolk.
- **If you prefer your yolk to be set, leave the egg in the water a bit longer.**
- If you want a really hard-boiled egg, leave it in the water for up to nine minutes.

- To be clear about what information examination questions are asking for
- To read different texts to find and use information
- To practise close reading texts for information

Close reading

TASK: Remind yourself of the task on page 6 before working through these pages.

Close-reading strategies

Close reading enables you to understand a text in detail, and select the information you need to answer a question. You should close read once you have found the relevant section by skimming or scanning. Many readers use a number of the following close-reading skills without even realising it.

- Read the text slowly, trying to understand what it means or the main ideas it is trying to put across. As you do this, annotate the text, noting relevant information.
- Try to work out the purpose of the text. If you understand why the writer has written a text, you will be better able to understand their viewpoint and what they are trying to say.
- Look for patterns – does the writer have the same viewpoint throughout the text? Do they change their opinions – and if so, where and why?
- Consider how the writer's ideas develop. Sometimes they might stack a number of similar ideas into one section, or they might use a new paragraph to explore each new idea.
- Ask questions while you are reading. Think about what questions you would like to ask the writer to help you understand what they have written. These might be:

PASS LEVEL 2 ✓ PASS LEVEL 2

In an examination, you can use a highlighter to indicate relevant points while you are reading a text. Then you will easily be able to find the information you need to answer the questions.

> What is the main message you want to get across?

> What are your views on this subject?

> Where did you get your information?

> Are there any other views you should consider?

ACTIVITY

1 Read the four questions in speech bubbles. Practise close reading the text in the article on the next page. As you read, imagine asking the writer the four questions. Jot down what you think the answers would be.

2 Now read the examination-style questions below. Use your reading skills to find the answers in the article.

a When was the last survey of children's sizes?
b How much taller is the average child today?
c What do the researchers hope the new furniture will lead to?
d Why do the researchers want ergonomically shaped chairs?
e Why are children suffering from back problems?
f What is the average weight for 16-year-old girls?

Schools buying stronger chairs as pupils get bigger

Growing up: pupils are larger

By **Laura Clark**

Schools are having to order reinforced chairs and higher tables as pupils get fatter and taller, it emerged yesterday.

Furniture suppliers who measured 1,400 pupils found they were more than an inch taller than those of a generation ago, and several pounds heavier.

The study, alongside similar checks in other European countries, led to the introduction of EU guidelines on school furniture.

All new fittings are expected to comply with the standard, which adds up to an inch to the dimensions of tables and chairs.

The last comparable survey of children's sizes took place in the 1970s.

The researchers said the new furniture should lead to better behaviour and attainment. Pupils squashed into small seats and desks are uncomfortable and fidget and misbehave, they said.

Youngsters' arms and legs are longer than they were in the 1970s and they are also rounder.

Levent Caglar, of the Furniture Industry Research Association, said the new standard backed the introduction of height-adjustable tables to provide extra leg room to fit in with children's growing limbs.

Chair legs are becoming sturdier and chair backs stronger to withstand greater force when children sit down, lean back or tip the chairs forward or back.

The new standard also calls for ergonomically shaped chairs to guard against damage to children's backs. Chiropractors have reported a sharp increase in complaints of back trouble among children which is thought to be caused by inactive lifestyles and hours spent slumped in front of the computer and TV.

Mr Caglar said: 'The last time children were measured was in 1971. The assumption was that children had not changed significantly since then.

'My study showed that children have been growing since 1971. In that time, they have grown another three centimetres, just over an inch, or one centimetre every decade.

'The greatest increase was in their legs. Their trunks were not really growing that much but legs were getting longer and longer.'

The average weight of 16-year-olds in the study was 10st 8lb for boys and 9st 6lb for girls.

New school furniture must pass tests of size, shape, strength and stability. Mr Caglar said: 'It means children can concentrate better, are less likely to fidget, are not distracted and behave much better.'

PASS LEVEL 2 ✓ PASS LEVEL 2

In an examination, always close read the questions before you read the text. This will help you to focus on locating the exact information required for your answer. Do not be afraid to state any obvious points and ideas from the text. The questions are designed so that you can find the answers readily in the text.

Peer/Self-assessment

Look back at the learning objectives. What can you now do confidently? What do you need to practise further?

TASK: To learn and practise summarising relevant information from texts in order to answer Functional Skills English examination-style questions.

Summarising

Summarising is the skill of extracting the main points of information from a text or texts and then connecting them into a short piece of writing. A good summary shows that you understand what you have read. In the examination, you may be asked to summarise only particular points from a text.

ACTIVITY

1 Read the question below together with the notes from the examiner explaining what the question is asking you to do.

'Summarise': the question tells you the reading skill you need to use. The question is in two parts – you need two parts to your summary.

'Problems' – you should only include information on problems in the first part of your summary. Ignore other information in the article.

A different focus for the second part – include only information about what people can do to protect themselves. Ignore other information.

Summarise:
- the problems caused by identity theft
- what people can do to protect themselves from it.

2 The first part of the text on the next page (How your identity can be stolen) has been highlighted and annotated to show you how to prepare a summary. Read the text and annotations carefully.

3 Read the student's summary of the first part of the text below. Has the student missed anything?

> **Identity theft**
> Identity theft is a problem where one in four people have been affected. If someone steals your identity they can apply for a passport, credit card and spend your money. People steal bank cards, passports or junk mail but look in your dustbin too.

Look out for questions that do not include the word 'summarise' but still require you to use your summarising skills. For example, you might be asked to 'write a brief document' based on some of the information in a text. This means you should summarise.

4 Write your own summary of the second part of the text (Keeping your identity safe). First, jot down key words and phrases. (In the examination, you could highlight the text.) Then write out all the key information in a shortened form. Check if you have missed anything.

PASS LEVEL 2 ✓

How your identity can be stolen

Identity theft is a growing problem, with more than one in four people claiming that they have either been a victim of crime or know someone who has. By stealing your identity, someone can illegally apply for a passport or a credit card. If they get their hands on your bank details, they'll also be able to use your money to buy goods for themselves.

Although your bank details are one of the most common things criminals look for, your identity can also be stolen through your passport, your driving licence and junk mail that you receive. You may think that you are keeping your details safe, but identity thieves have also been known to go through dustbins to look for receipts that you've thrown away.

You may not find out that your identity has been stolen until you try to apply for a credit card and you're told that you already owe money to a number of companies. You could also find out if you apply for benefits and are told that you seem to be already claiming them.

Keeping your identity safe

Your identity and personal details are as valuable to criminals as your mobile phone and your wallet, so you should take the same amount of care to protect them. As well as using your common sense to keep your cards and passwords safe, there are more specific ways you can protect your details:

- Rip up, shred or burn your receipts safely before you throw them away to make sure your card number cannot be seen.

- If you're about to go to university, don't change your address with your bank until you're happy that your personal mail will be safe.

- If you've just moved, set up a mail re-direct with the Post Office for at least a year. This will make sure that all your mail will be sent to your new address automatically – you should also change your address with your bank and other companies as soon as possible.

©Crown Copyright

> Headings can give you the main idea of each part of the text.

> Highlighting key words and phrases helps you start to create a visual summary. Remember to highlight only the key points, or those that are asked for in the question.

My learning objectives ▼

- To be clear about what examination questions are asking for
- To practise summarising different viewpoints
- To practise comparing different viewpoints

KEY TERM

A **viewpoint** is a person's opinion.

Summarising different viewpoints

In some questions you might be asked to summarise two different points of view. When you are highlighting and summarising the main points, it is a good idea to separate the two **viewpoints**. You could use two different coloured highlighters to help you.

ACTIVITY 1

Look at the article opposite about two girls who committed insurance fraud. The main points relating to the views of their parents have been highlighted.

1 Summarise the parents' viewpoint, using the highlighted points. Aim to write about 50 words.

2 Read the rest of the article closely. Note down the views of the author, Bryony Gordon.

3 Write a brief summary of Bryony's different viewpoint on the girls' story.

Comparing viewpoints

You could be asked to compare viewpoints from one or more texts. Read the short extract below, taken from a different article on the same subject.

PASS LEVEL 2 ✓

You might be asked to summarise viewpoints or opinions into a short piece of writing, a table or a chart: follow the instructions very carefully to produce exactly what the question asks for. Do not add your own opinions unless you are asked to do so.

> Their lawyer, Renato Tonini: "They are very nervous and scared. The prison is very unpleasant and unhealthy. They are sleeping on the floor with no mattresses because the prison is so over-crowded. It is very hard for them …"

ACTIVITY 2

1 Compare the viewpoints of Bryony Gordon and Renato Tonini. First summarise what each says about the girls' situation. What does Bryony Gordon imagine their months in Brazil will be like? How does Renato Tonini describe their actual experience?

2 Once you have completed your summaries you need to decide: what is the best way to present this information for a reader?

Steps to successful summarising

1 Skim the text to understand the main ideas and views the writer is trying to put across.

2 Close read the text for additional information. This might include the writer's purpose, viewpoint, different opinions or even facts that you missed when skimming.

3 Highlight the main points that are relevant to the question or task.

4 Connect the ideas and information you have selected together in a clear, short summary.

WHY SHOULD ANYONE FEEL SORRY FOR THESE SPOILT, STUPID GIRLS?

By Bryony Gordon

British tourists Shanti Simone Andrews, right, and Rebecca Claire Turner speak before receiving their sentences in court in Rio de Janeiro.

I am finding it difficult to feel sorry for Shanti Andrews and Rebecca Turner, no matter how hard I try. To recap, they are two British 23-year-olds who decided, upon graduating, to fly off on a nine-month tour of the world, taking in over 30 countries. To Asia, Australia and South America they went, finishing in Brazil, where they took it upon themselves to commit insurance fraud.

They got caught out, chucked in prison, and were this week told that their world tour would be extended by almost a year and a half, when a judge in Rio gave them 16 months' community service. This will probably be spent cleaning *favelas*, teaching English and reading to children in orphanages.

They sobbed at this news, as if they themselves were little orphan Annies and not two privileged women who could afford a university education, and then the luxury of putting off work to go on what was essentially a vastly extended holiday. Two women who – and you're not going to believe this – had just graduated in *law*, a qualification that they obviously felt put them above it.

At the time of their arrest, Shanti's father, Alan, had this to say: 'Of all the countries on their list, I particularly didn't want them to go to Brazil. I'd read so much about the crime and corruption.' Yes, some of which was committed by your daughter and her chum. But I digress. I must let Alan continue. 'I think the lesson to tell your children if they insist on going round the world is, "Be very careful."' Actually, I think I'd say this: 'Darling, please don't try and hoodwink the authorities into believing that some local has stolen your iPod and your digital camera when they have not. This will make you look like a spoilt and greedy European and they will rightfully throw the book at you.'

Not these parents, though. Upon hearing of the sentence, Shanti's mother, Simone Headley, said this: 'It's going to be a long time before they fly back home. Their lives are potentially ruined.'

I mean, really? If their lives have been ruined, then they have only themselves to blame. *They* put their future careers on the line when they decided to commit insurance fraud, not the police, who were simply doing their jobs.

Andrews and Turner may not have murdered anyone, but their arrogance is pretty criminal. It's nothing out of the ordinary, though. Apparently, this fake insurance scam is popular among backpackers who want to finance their trips home, having squandered their cash on cheap booze at full moon parties, hair braiding, friendship bracelets and whatever else it is that these people do as they trot around the globe 'finding themselves'.

I know that many people on gap years set out with noble intentions to do charity work, but in a recent interview, the development economist Peter Griffiths said that 'the Third World does not need recent graduates who want to learn their job by experimenting on them. You are a drain on their economies unless you are truly a world expert.' Oh well. Perhaps as they sweep the slums of Rio, Shanti Andrews and Rebecca Turner will realise how lucky they are, and that the real world isn't all it's cracked up to be.

My learning objectives ▼

- To be clear about what information examination questions are asking for
- To be able to read several texts and summarise what I have read
- To practise summarising information from more than one text

Summarising information from different texts

In the examination, you may be asked to gather information from several sources and then put the main ideas into one summary. Gathering information could also be the first step in comparing texts.

ACTIVITY 1

1 Read the examination-style task below.

Summarise the points given in the two articles on how to prevent identity theft.

2 Read each article in turn and list the advice given.
3 Summarise your notes.

Comparing texts

In the examination, you may be asked to compare different texts. You will usually be given a list of things to focus on. You should use your summarising skills to prepare and write comparisons.

ACTIVITY 2

Compare the two texts on identity theft.
Think about similarities and differences in:

- Purpose – why the writers wrote their texts.
- Viewpoint – what the writers think about identity theft.
- Layout – how they each set out their articles.
- Content – what they say, and how they say it.
- Personal experience – what has happened to the two writers?

PASS LEVEL 2 ✔

Make sure you do *exactly* what the question asks for. For this question:

- Include all the key points from both articles. Make sure you do not write down the same point twice.
- There are 10 marks allocated, so you should include 10 points. Checking the number of possible marks will always help you to work out how much to write.

Peer/Self-assessment

Look back at the learning objectives. Which summarising skills can you now use accurately and confidently? Which skills need further practice?

checkmyfile

About us | Jargon Buster | Site map | Contact us

Take control of your personal information

| Home | Check your Credit Report | Free Credit Score | Find a Lender | Debt Advice Centre |

Identity theft: identity thieves target MySpace and Facebook By Richard Catlin

Using social networking sites could place you at an increased risk of falling victim to identity theft.

Apparently benign websites are likely to be trawled by identity thieves. Consumer-facing websites such as *FriendsReunited* and *WAYN* and business networking sites such as *LinkedIn* and *ecademy* each contain a wealth of personal information that is presented in a user-friendly format from a criminal's point of view.

Armed with just a few personal details that are listed with personal profiles on these sites, criminals may well have enough information to steal an identity.

Many users freely list vital details including their date of birth, where they grew up and where they currently live. With just a small amount of further digging, all entirely lawfully, an identity thief could obtain a copy of your birth certificate directly from a government website for just £10.

From this, and possibly being able to find your full home address simply by looking on a local phone or electoral register, the possibility of obtaining credit in your name is a much more realistic threat.

Tips to help protect yourself if you use these sites: you should use a nickname or different spelling of your name, use a completely different date of birth at least 3 months different to your real one (not just a day or so out as some commentators have recently advised) and in every case, always cite consistently an incorrect current location.

We also believe that the risks of using *FriendsReunited* far outweigh the benefits: you can unsubscribe by following the links to the privacy policy found at the foot of the homepage.

Stop ID fraud

Real Life Identity Theft – Mr A

Mr A, 40, had £9,000 taken out of his accounts by criminals. Mr A suspects that the criminals got hold of his details from a number of statements he threw away the week prior to the identity fraud.

Mr A now has to answer extra security questions in order to get information on all his accounts. However, the same bank was sent a fraudulent letter asking for Mr A's address to be changed. It seemed the criminals were not stopping there, as another bank informed Mr A the following month that someone had attempted to open a new account in his name online.

Mr A is now very careful when disposing of his letters, making sure he shreds anything with his name and address or personal details, and also makes sure all his accounts are monitored.

Key piece of advice from Mr A: 'Always be aware of what transactions are going through your account, even if that means saving every single receipt you have. Straight after the incident I bought a shredder so that I could get rid of my letters safely. Another thing I have found very useful is to check my credit rating on a regular basis. This way you are made aware of any other addresses or accounts that are linked to you.'

Different purposes of texts

TASK: To learn and practise a range of reading skills in identifying the purpose and commenting on the effectiveness of texts in order to answer Functional Skills English examination-style questions.

Peer/Self-assessment

Look at the learning objectives. Think about what you can do confidently, and what you still need to learn or practise to achieve Level 2.

Understanding different purposes

To achieve a Level 2 in Reading, you must be able to read a text and understand exactly why it was written – its purpose. For example, the writer might be trying to make you think or feel a certain way about a specific issue, or they might simply be giving you instructions on how to do something. Each text may have a number of different purposes.

ACTIVITY 1

1 Look at the range of purposes for writing in the table below.

Purpose	Definition
Persuade	To encourage the reader to share the writer's views or to act as the writer wishes
Inform	To give facts to the reader
Instruct	To give knowledge to the reader so that they can carry out a task
Explain	To help the reader to understand something

PASS LEVEL 2 ✓

Practise reading texts and working out their purposes. If you understand why a text was written, it will help you to comment on how effective it is.

2 Discuss and jot down any other purposes for writing that you can think of.
3 Write clear definitions of the purposes you have thought of, and enter them into a table like the one above.

Identifying different purposes

To work out the purpose of a text you have to consider what it is trying to do and what it aims to achieve. The text below is a job advertisement. Its purpose is both to provide information on the job and to persuade readers to apply for it.

ACTIVITY 2

1 What parts of the advert indicate its purpose is to inform?
2 What features show its purpose is also to persuade?

Do you have what it takes in the fashion stakes?

Fresh Fashion

Here at Fresh Fashion we are looking for that special person to join our exceptional sales team. You will greet customers, give advice and information about products and services, and help with any enquiries. We will give you a generous discount on clothing and weekly sales bonuses, as well as a £6 per hour starting salary.

Location: Central Manchester Hours: Saturday 9 am–5.30 pm

Future fashion stars should apply to the Manager, Fresh Fashion.

ACTIVITY 3

1 Look at the texts below. Identify the purpose of each one. To do this, think about:
   - Clues in the content – what is the writing telling you? What actions might you take after reading?
   - Clues in the language – are the words and phrases simple, factual, persuasive, **emotive**, and so on?
   - Clues in the layout and any images.

> **KEY TERM**
>
> **Emotive** language appeals to your emotions e.g. love, hate, fear.

Setting up your new computer

Step 1: Unpack the monitor and tower. Plug the monitor into the back of the tower. Unpack and connect the keyboard and mouse.

Step 2: Plug the monitor and tower into your surge protector strip. Next, power on the monitor and then the tower. Once the system is powered up, you can begin customising your computer.

Step 3: Follow the instructions for customising Windows. Enter your product key, name the computer, and create an administrator password. Then set the date and time.

Step 4: Once Windows is up and running, you can connect your printer, network, and any other devices.

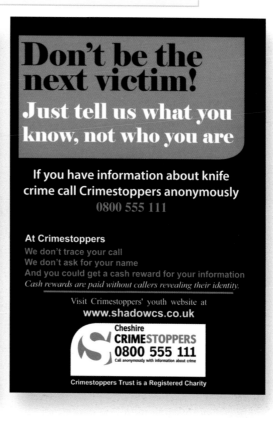

Don't be the next victim!

Just tell us what you know, not who you are

If you have information about knife crime call Crimestoppers anonymously
0800 555 111

At Crimestoppers
We don't trace your call
We don't ask for your name
And you could get a cash reward for your information
Cash rewards are paid without callers revealing their identity.

Visit Crimestoppers' youth website at
www.shadowcs.co.uk

Cheshire
CRIMESTOPPERS
0800 555 111
Call anonymously with information about crime

Crimestoppers Trust is a Registered Charity

My learning objectives ▼

- To understand how the use of facts and opinions can help to identify the purpose of a text
- To understand how facts and opinions may be used to convey meaning
- To begin to comment on how effectively texts convey their meaning

Fact and opinion

Once you can recognise the purpose of a text, you can start to identify how effectively the writer has managed to achieve that purpose. One way is to study the use of **facts** and **opinions** in a text.

ACTIVITY 1

1 Read the following text – its purpose is to inform. List the facts included in it.

'EastEnders' nominated for 166 British Soap Awards

Posted by Special magazine 10th December 2009 16.20

Tags British soap awards | EastEnders

'EastEnders' was first screened by the BBC in 1985 and was originally shown twice a week. It is set in Albert Square in a fictional area of London called Walford. The soap has been nominated for 166 British Soap Awards.

Rate this story: ★ ★ ★ ★ ★   Average rating: ★ ★ ★ (13 votes)

2 Now read a different version of the text, below. It has an additional purpose – to persuade the reader to agree that 'EastEnders' is fabulous. List the opinions that have been added to it.

The fabulous TV show 'EastEnders' first burst onto our screens in 1985 and was originally screened twice a week. Thankfully, we now have the opportunity to watch this captivating show almost every day. It's an explosive social drama, set in Albert Square in a fictional area of London called Walford. The increasingly popular soap has been nominated for 166 British Soap Awards and I believe it should have won them all!

3 How do the opinions add to the effectiveness of the text?

ACTIVITY 2

The writer of the newspaper article on the next page has included a great deal of factual information.

1 Scan the article to find ten facts.

2 Discuss how the inclusion of the facts adds to the effectiveness of the article.

KEY TERMS

A **fact** is something real or true that can be proven or backed up with evidence. For example, it is a fact that there are 24 hours in one day.

An **opinion** is based on a writer's own views or beliefs and cannot be proven as true. For example, it is an opinion that British weather is the worst in the world.

In factual texts, look out for references to research, polls, surveys, experts, numbers and statistics. They all add to the effectiveness of the text by suggesting that the information is based on hard evidence.

Opinions are just based on the writer's thoughts and are not backed up with evidence – but they can be persuasive and entertaining.

A mobile, the gizmo we just can't live without

By **Sophie Borland**

Ringing endorsement for mobiles

If you sometimes wonder how you ever got by without a mobile, you're in good company.

For it's been voted the household item that has most changed our lives.

According to a poll, more than a quarter of us think the mobile is the gadget that has altered our behaviour the most.

And for the young, it's even more important. Of those aged 16–24, 42 per cent named it as their favourite life-changing gadget.

The mobile came in ahead of the laptop – and the MP3 player – in the list compiled by consumer website which.co.uk.

Digital cameras and satellite navigation systems also proved popular. And although hair straighteners, relied upon by many women to remove their kinks and curls, came in at 11th, the TV was ranked just 19th.

But not all gadgets improve our lives, the poll found. The foot spa was named the most useless gadget. And the bread maker came close behind – most said they rarely used theirs.

Neither did many think ice cream makers, orange peelers and electronic carving knives are worth keeping in the cupboard.

But phones are crucial for modern life, it appears – and not just for keeping in touch with friends and family.

One of those polled by consumer website which.co.uk, said: 'My phone stores my entire address book and calendar, backs it up and synchronises it at work and at home on my computers.'

Today, there are more than 3.3 billion mobiles in the world. Britain has one of the highest rates of ownership. Last month, dozens queued outside shops when Apple's latest iPhone was released. It has high-speed Internet access as well as more standard features such as a camera.

Jess Ross, editor of the Which? website, said: 'Forget games consoles and TVs, we've found that the mobile phone is the gadget that people say has changed their life. As the popularity of the iPhone has shown, the multi-functional mobile is worth queuing around the block for.'

Satnavs were also described as invaluable by those polled. One said: 'TomTom satnav – it took us cross-country to the airport when the motorway was at a standstill.

'This saved us the price of buying new plane tickets to get home and therefore earned its keep immediately!'

Washing machines, vacuum cleaners and microwaves all ranked in the top ten. And even the salad spinner earned its place in the rankings. One of those surveyed said theirs had revolutionised their life.

But not everyone is convinced of the importance of gadgets. Half of those polled who were over 65, said they could not identify a particular item that they felt had made a real difference to their lives.

Last year, hair straighteners were voted women's favourite gadget in a poll for the electronics chain Comet.

My learning objectives ▼

- To be clear about what examination questions on meaning and effectiveness are asking for
- To understand how writers convey meaning
- To understand and comment on how effectively meaning is conveyed

What makes texts effective?

Conveying meaning

The language used, as well as graphs, diagrams, pictures and layout, all contribute to the meaning of a text. To judge the effectiveness of a text, you should first consider what the writer's purpose for writing was, and then decide how well all the features of the text work together in conveying meaning and achieving that purpose.

ACTIVITY 1

Read the examination-style question below, asking you to comment on the effectiveness of a text. Study the examiner's annotations – they will help you to understand exactly what you need to do to achieve Level 2.

> The bullet points tell you what to cover. Make sure you write a paragraph on each one.

> The purpose of the text is stated – to tell adults how to keep children safe and persuade them to do so. Keep the two purposes in mind as you read and assess the text.

In the text on the right, the writer tells us how to keep children safe and persuades us to do so. **How effective is the text?**

You should look at:

> Content – this means what is actually said. Is the content clear and relevant?

- the content and language
- the layout
- the picture and what it adds to the text.

> Layout – this means the way the text is presented. Comment on any headings, numbering, bold text, and so on. How does it help to make the text clear and persuasive?

> Picture – state what or who is in the picture and how the image contributes to the meaning and purpose of the text.

> Language – this means the words used. Is it clear and persuasive? Quote some of the words used to back up your opinion.

> The question asks you to decide how effective the text is – this means how well it achieves the stated purpose. Make sure you look at all the features listed before coming to your decision, and refer to all of them in explaining your view of the text.

ACTIVITY 2

1 Make a plan for an answer to the question. Use the examiner's annotations to help you. Remember, you are looking for points that make the text effective in its purposes of giving people information on how to keep children safe and persuading them to do so.
   a Decide on at least three points to make about the content of the text.
   b Decide on at least three points to make about the layout of the text.
   c Jot down two points to make about the picture.
2 Thinking about the points you have listed, decide how effective you think the text is. Make brief notes.
3 Draft your answer. Use all the points in your plan.
4 Check your work against the examiner's notes above. Have you included everything you need to? Have you given your own opinion on how effective the text is, and why?

> **PASS LEVEL 2** ✓
>
> Use key words from the question in your answer. This will show the examiner you are focusing on the question – and will help you not to miss out something you have been asked to do.

KEEPING CHILDREN SAFE

As a parent, it is vital that you take every opportunity to teach your child how to be safe. As soon as you can, it is sensible to teach them their full name, address and telephone number. Repeat these with them until you're sure they can remember. It is a good idea to make this fun to help them remember!

▲ Start teaching children how to be safe as soon as they are able to understand. Tell them never to go off with anyone, not even someone they know, without first asking you or the adult who is looking after them.

▲ Never leave young children on their own in unsupervised areas, even playgrounds or parks. Never leave them alone in the car or outside a shop, it only takes an instant for a child to disappear.

▲ Children under eight years old shouldn't be out unsupervised, especially in busy towns or at night. Even when playing out close to home, they should be monitored and in sight of an adult or a much older child.

▲ If you're in a busy area, keep children in a pram or buggy, hold their hands tightly, or use reins so they can't wander off. Don't walk far ahead of small children who can't keep up and always keep a close eye on them. It only takes seconds for toddlers to wander off.

▲ Teach children safe ways to cross the road (making fun rules can really help here). Let them practise these with you until you are sure that they have understood. Don't allow them to cross busy roads unsupervised and they should never play near main roads.

▲ If you have taken your child to a busy or new place, you should arrange somewhere safe to meet in case you get separated. Make sure that children know what to do if they ever get lost, and who is safest to ask for help – a police officer, shop assistant or other people with young children.

▲ Always find time to sit down and chat to your children on a regular basis, this will help them feel comfortable if they ever need to confide in you. Listen to your children, especially when they are trying to tell you about things that worry them. Is there a bully at school or a babysitter they don't like? Is there something about an activity they attend that makes them uncomfortable? Never get cross or frustrated with them when they are talking to you about important things and try to give sensible advice.

Always remember:

A child is happiest when they feel secure and loved. They need to know they can always come to you if they are feeling threatened, uncomfortable or unhappy.

Top tips for coping with independent children:

1 Always find out where they are going
2 Always find out who they will be with
3 Always encourage them to take their phone and keep in touch with you if their plans change
4 Always be willing to collect them if they are left alone.

Peer/Self-assessment

Look back at the learning objectives. What can you do well? What do you need to practise further?

Point of view, implicit meaning and bias

TASK: To learn about **point of view**, **implicit meaning** and **bias**. To practise detecting these in texts in order to answer Functional Skills English exam-style questions.

What does the writer really mean?

Detecting a writer's point of view may not be straightforward – writers do not always say what they mean directly. Sometimes they use clues in their language to suggest what they really mean.

Reading between the lines

'Point of view' is the writer's opinion.

'Implicit meaning' is meaning that is implied – it is not stated directly, but suggested in the writer's use of language.

'Bias' is when a writer conveys only their own point of view.

Looking for the writer's point of view, implicit meaning and bias is often called 'reading between the lines'. Here are some things to look for when reading between the lines.

'That's an interesting top. Pink and orange – different.'

What does the speaker really mean?

The source	Who wrote the text? Are they likely to have a particular point of view?
Humour	Does the writer use humour to get across their 'real' message? For example, 'Revision – it's great, but I'd rather pull out my own toenails with tweezers.' What does the writer really think?
Sarcasm	This is saying the opposite of what is really meant. For example, 'Well, you lot have been fun to teach today.' What does this teacher really mean?
Facts or figures	A writer can choose to mention only those facts and figures that back up their point of view. For example, 'Sixty per cent of people think our service is excellent'. But what about the views of the other forty per cent? Vague figures may be used for effect – can they be proven?
Opinion	A writer might simply state their opinion as if it is a fact. For example, 'I believe that our service is excellent.' Can their opinion be trusted?
Authority	Writers might suggest their own authority by using words like, 'Of course …' or 'Don't we all …' to imply that everyone agrees with them.
Italics	'Did Tom arrive first?' is a straightforward question, but 'Did Tom *really* arrive first?' implies disbelief.
Emphasis or repetition of key words	Emphasising or repeating key words can encourage the reader to pay more attention to those words. For example, 'Global warming will devastate our world, devastate our lives and devastate our children's future.'

ACTIVITY

Look at the texts below.

1 What is the stated purpose of the Travel Safe leaflet?
2 Try to read between the lines. Think about the points listed – how does the writer of the leaflet get across their point of view? Give examples.
3 What do you think another purpose of the leaflet might be?
4 What do you think Jeremy Clarkson really thinks about the school sports day?
5 How does he use humour, opinion and sarcasm to get his point of view across?

TRAVEL
SAFE

BRITISH
TRANSPORT
POLICE

Millions of people travel every day
very few **become victims of crime**

Fear of crime is as much of a problem as crime itself. There are many simple precautions you can take to increase your confidence and make it even less likely you will become a crime victim.

Crime You are actually very safe when travelling by rail. Crime is not common and violent crime is rare (there is about 1 reported crime for every 300,000 passenger journeys). Women are not usually the victims of violent crime.

My eldest daughter is not sleek. In fact, to be brutally honest, she has the aerodynamic properties of a bungalow and the coordination of an American bombing raid.

She puts a huge effort into running. Her arms and legs flail around like the Flying Scotsman's pistons but despite this you need a theodolite to ascertain that she is actually moving forwards. She's a bit of a duffer at the school's sports day.

Luckily, the school tries to operate a strict 'no competition' rule. The game starts, the children exert energy and then the game finishes. This doesn't work terribly well with the 50-metre running race but often there are never any winners and consequently there are never any losers.

Analysing language

Point of view

Looking at the source and purpose of a text can help you to detect point of view.

ACTIVITY 1

1 What is the purpose of the leaflet on the next page?
2 Who wrote the leaflet? What bias would you expect in their point of view?
3 Find examples of the writer using each of the following to get across their viewpoint effectively.

Humour – making something sound funny	Opinion – stating opinion as fact	Italics/bold/highlighting for emphasis

Facts and figures – using facts that support their argument	Sarcasm – saying the opposite of what they really mean

Repetition of key words to make the reader pay attention to them	Authority – suggesting that everyone agrees by using a **rhetorical question**

KEY TERM

A **rhetorical question** is a question that is not meant to be answered but suggests the reader must agree.

Emotive language

Emotive language causes people to feel emotional. It may be used to get across a point of view and to persuade readers to share the writer's opinion.

ACTIVITY 2

1 Put these groups of words in order from the least emotive to the most.

nice   OK   amazing

horrific   bad   awful

irritated   devastated   upset

2 Rewrite these sentences, replacing the word in bold with another from its group. What is the effect on the writing?

The food was **OK**.

The scene at the accident was **bad**.

She was **irritated** by her poor exam results.

3 Find at least five examples of emotive language in the leaflet on the next page. What effect are they likely to have on the reader?

Be smart. Don't start.

There are loads of reasons to stay smoke-free. Here are just some of them.

1 Live longer

Many smokers die before their time. On average 5.5 minutes of life is lost for every cigarette smoked. That's half a day a week for the average smoker. Many smokers die up to 25 years earlier than they should. Smoking is like committing suicide slowly and painfully.

2 Keep your looks

Some people think smoking makes you look older. Well sure it does – your skin gets wrinkled before it should and your complexion dulls. Teeth and fingers are stained a horrible yellow-brown and gums are more susceptible to unsightly diseases, like gingivitis.

© GASP Smoke Free Solutions

3 Cash not ash

A 20-a-day smoker spends around £2000 a year. Surely there are better things to spend your cash on. Clothes, CDs, holidays, computers, anything in fact. And that £2000 is an investment in an early death! Crazy isn't it?

4 Don't get nasty diseases

"Smoking is bad for your health." That has to be one of the biggest understatements of the century. A cigarette contains 4,000 chemicals. Nasties like carbon monoxide, tar, arsenic, ammonia and hydrogen cyanide. Smokers die of heart attacks and lung cancer. And worse! Try emphysema – a terrible disease that rots the lungs, making breathing a real struggle. Dying from emphysema is like drowning slowly.

5 Stay fit and active

The carbon monoxide in cigarette smoke robs the system of oxygen. Smoking also increases heart rate and narrows blood vessels. That means smokers have less stamina. So if you're into sport, cigarettes are a big No-No. 20-year-old smokers have the same fitness levels as 35-year-old non-smokers. Also, smokers can't fight off infections so easily. They're more susceptible to coughs, colds, flu, ear infections, etc.

ACTIVITY 3

Use the examples you found in the text to answer this exam-style question:

> How does the writer of the leaflet use language to persuade the reader not to smoke?

If you are asked to focus on language and how it is used by the writer, make sure you:

- always use a quote so the examiner can see which words you are focusing on
- always explain why a specific word has been used
- never write down a technical term (e.g. rhetorical question) without explaining how the use of the term contributes to the text's effectiveness.

PASS LEVEL 2

27

- To be clear about what 'analyse', 'audience needs' and 'respond' mean
- To understand what a 'respond' examination question is asking me to do
- To practise a range of reading skills in analysing and responding to texts

Peer/Self-assessment

Look at the learning objectives. Think about what you can do confidently, and what you need to learn or practise.

Read and respond to articles

TASK: To answer this Functional Skills English examination-style question:

You have a friend who is concerned about their hearing. Read the articles opposite and write a factsheet that would be useful to people like your friend. Include the information you have read on what is causing deafness in Britain today, and what they should do to avoid hearing problems.

To achieve a Level 2 in Reading, you must be able to read a text and think about why an audience might want to read it. You should then respond actively to its contents. This means that you have to do something after you have read the text. For example, you might have to:

- read and follow a set of instructions
- read for the information you need to solve a 'real-life' problem
- read a letter of complaint and respond to the issues raised in it
- use the information in the text to answer an examination question.

For the reading question you have been set on these pages, you have to read for information and present your findings as a factsheet. Work through the activity below to use a range of reading skills to complete the task.

In the examination, look at how many marks the question is worth to help you decide how many things to write down.

Put the information into your own words but don't change the meaning of what you are writing. Do not add your own points – this question is a test of how well you can read, not how well you can invent advice!

ACTIVITY

1. Read the question carefully and decide exactly what information you need to find.
2. Consider the two texts: why might someone need to read them?
3. Skim the first article for the main ideas – it has already been highlighted to help you to do this. Then read it closely for the information you need and make notes.
4. Do the same for the second article.
5. Look at the information you have generated. Some points may be mentioned in both articles, but you only need to include them once.
6. Re-read the question to remind yourself of the format your answer should be in. (You will sometimes be given a suggested layout for your answer). Then write your answer.

iPod creating a 'deaf generation'

Our love affair with the iPod (or indeed other brands of MP3 player) could see **today's children go deaf up to 30 years earlier than their parent**s, according to recent research.

Deafness Research UK is concerned that children may face deafness at a young age because they listen to their MP3 players too loudly. The theory is based on a national UK survey conducted by the charity, which found that 1-in-3 (38 per cent) of 16–34 year olds don't understand that listening to loud music on a personal music player can damage their hearing, as can going to loud bars or gigs, playing loud music in the car or working with machinery.

Ringing in the ears, or tinnitus, is a sign of damage to your hearing. Vivienne Michael, Chief Executive of Deafness Research UK says, "More than a third of people who have experienced tinnitus after listening to loud music are people who listen to their MP3 player every day, and 14 per cent of people we surveyed spend up to 28 hours a week listening to their music player. Yet many of the young people regularly using their MP3 players for long periods of time are frighteningly unaware of the fact that it can permanently damage your hearing".

What can children do to protect their hearing?

More and more young people are listening to music through MP3 players, but at high volumes these can cause hearing loss. The maximum volume personal music players can reach is 100 dBA – which is above the danger level.

Repeated exposure to music from personal music players, through headphones, at, or near to, maximum volume will be sufficient to cause permanent damage to hearing in some people. As a rule, if other people can hear the sound from a personal music player, then it is too loud.

It is recommended that even if the volume on a personal music player is at about 60 per cent of maximum (manufacturer's settings), it shouldn't be listened to for more than an hour continuously a day.

Tips for the younger generation

- Turn down the volume on your music players, whether personal or hi-fi.
- Take ear plugs when you are going to a club or party.
- Be aware of how long you spend playing loud video games.
- Lower the volume of your mobile phone's ringtone.

My learning objectives ▼

- To be clear about what 'analyse', 'audience needs' and 'respond' mean
- To practise a range of reading skills in actively responding to texts

Read and respond to a letter

To answer this Functional Skills English examination-style question:

The following letter was printed in your local newspaper. The author has clear views about the behaviour of young people. Write a reply to the letter, responding to each of the points he makes, putting across your own views.

Read

Dear Editor

I read your article about 'Terrific Teenagers' (11 October) and I couldn't agree less. I live in a small seaside town and have been fearful of young people for a number of years. I would like to raise the following concerns:

Firstly, teenagers are given too much money and too much freedom to do what they like. They do not use their money and freedom carefully and responsibly.

Secondly, most parents seem to have little or no control over their children.

It seems teenagers have no respect for authority, including their own parents and teachers, so it is no wonder that most do what they like, when they like.

In fact, I recently heard a police chief say her first concern was the safety of her own officers. I feel that the police have too few powers to control teenagers, and most are frightened by big groups of youths.

Finally, most teenagers have no respect for themselves. This itself has caused a drastic increase in teenage pregnancies, unruly behaviour, and a total loss of control for many young people.

I realise this might sound as if I hate all young people, but that is simply not the case. I just think that most of them need much more discipline and much less freedom.

Yours faithfully

Frank Thompson, 76

Remember, your task is to read and respond. Do not get distracted by making your own new points. Instead, focus on making sure you have answered all the points raised. For this question, 'Frank Thompson' makes five points and then states his conclusion. You must respond to each of these points to achieve top marks.

ACTIVITY 1

Close read the letter. Make brief notes of the key points you need to reply to. For example:

1 Too much money/freedom. Don't use responsibly.

In the examination, you could highlight or underline the key points to save time. This would give you a clear list of the relevant points in the right order.

Respond

ACTIVITY 2

1 Remember to write your answer in the correct format – in this case, a letter. Use the correct salutation (e.g. Dear Madam/Sir).

2 Start your letter with a clear introduction. State why you are writing, and make your own opinions about the letter written by Frank Thompson very clear.

3 Respond to each of the points you have noted. Use the key words from Frank Thompson's letter when you respond to each point. For example:

I do not feel that teenagers are given too much money and freedom...

Make sure you include a clear response to each of the issues raised – don't just say that you disagree, explain why.

4 Finish with a clear conclusion where you sum up your views.

5 Use the correct sign off.

Peer/Self-assessment

Look back at your finished letter. What have you done well? What needs further improvement? Make corrections to your letter if you need to.

enjoy

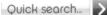

Nintendo Wii Fit – Why buy one?

Gaming is a multi billion dollar industry that continues to grow at an incredible rate. Twenty years ago people were playing on very basic games such as Pac Man and Hopper, and now you can play virtual ice hockey in your own front room!

So what is the Wii Fit? The Wii Fit is a games console that aims firstly to make you aware of your own fitness and then to help you get fit while having fun. There are a range of different accessories that can help you exercise such as the Balance Board and the Motion Plus accessories and they are all designed to help optimise your physique. The exercises have a range of benefits and help users to improve balance and posture, change their Body Mass Index, increase muscle tone and definition, or even to relax.

Wii Fit has an ever increasing range of physical exercises that you can enjoy from the comfort of your own home. There are four broad training categories with a range of different exercises in each. For those wishing to simply burn calories, there are a number of aerobic exercises which really improve cardiovascular levels. A range of balance games help to improve posture and balance. Muscle Workouts have been specially designed for those who wish to bulk up but not go to an expensive gym to do so. Those who wish to stretch and relax can enjoy yoga poses. Within these categories you will literally find everything from step aerobics and boxercise to snowboarding and skiing, rhythm boxing to bowling and jogging. There really is something for everyone.

To help you monitor your progress and fitness levels, there is a Wii Fit Channel where up to eight people can store and compare their personal fitness profiles. When you make progress in your fitness it is clearly tracked on your own personalised graph. Is Wii Fit the future of gaming? Is Wii Fit the future for exercise? We don't know, but it certainly brings a lot of fun on the way.

The Nintendo Wii – A Disaster Waiting to Happen?

By **Stuart Horsfield**

People in the UK today seem to be gripped by Nintendo Wii fever. Forget a kick around with your mates, kids are playing football on the latest Nintendo edition of the Premiership.

Forget socialising, you've got entertainment on the Nintendo Wii. In fact, forget most activities that involve quality communication. My teenage kids love their Nintendo Wii – but I just can't understand their enthusiasm.

So what does the Wii have to offer?

According to some it can reduce weight, increase fitness and improve social skills. What rubbish! It encourages children to miss out on sleep and can cause anxiety and illness – children spending more time indoors suffer more colds, headaches and eye strain. Critics of the Wii claim it will cause violence on British streets as people learn to enjoy fighting.

Now local authorities have come up with a plan to introduce gaming in schools. What about the kids who would rather enjoy a 'real' team sport with their mates? Fresh air costs nothing and is vital for good health – but the only way schools can afford the Wii is by selling off their playing fields.

Safety issues

The Wii is not as safe as Nintendo makes out either. Ask any physiotherapist and they will groan in horror at 'Nintendo whiplash', twisted shoulders, sprained ankles, neck injuries and countless bruises. More serious injuries range from dangerously swollen eyes to dislocated shoulders, serious hand wounds (one man sliced his hand as he tried to hit a virtual tennis ball) and back pain.

All this talk of exercise has made me fancy a walk. Unfortunately, as I hear the grunts of virtual tennis from the sitting room, I guess I'll be on my own in the fresh air.

IF NOT USED PROPERLY, THE NINTENDO WII CAN CAUSE A RANGE OF SERIOUS INJURIES.

BUY A COPY OF 'WII SAFETY' TODAY, BEFORE IT'S TOO LATE!

Paper 1

(40 marks)

In this paper you will be assessed for your reading and understanding skills. You will need to use the Resource Materials 'Nintendo Wii Fit – Why buy one?', 'The Nintendo Wii – A Disaster Waiting to Happen?' and 'Wii Safety'.

Your friend is hoping to buy a Nintendo Wii. Read the Resource Materials to find out about it.

The web page 'Nintendo Wii Fit – Why buy one?' is intended to inform readers about the product.

The article 'The Nintendo Wii – A Disaster Waiting to Happen?' has been written by a parent who does not understand the appeal and has concerns about it.

The advertisement for 'Wii Safety' is about injuries that could occur while using it.

1 Summarise the benefits of Wii Fit as described in the web page. [5]

2 What different physical activities can you try on a Wii Fit? Give your answer as a list of bullet points. [5]

3 What is the purpose of this Wii Fit web page? Give reasons to support your answer. [5]

4 Using the first two paragraphs of the article, describe how Stuart Horsfield feels about Nintendo gaming.
   Make sure you use evidence to support your ideas. [5]

5 In the article, how does Stuart Horsfield make it clear that he thinks gaming is dangerous? Use the following headings in your response:

   • Social issues

   • Health issues

   • Other dangers [10]

6 Your friend is thinking of buying a Nintendo Wii. Use the three resource materials to compile an information sheet on the advantages and disadvantages of buying a Wii.
   Write a paragraph about the advantages and a paragraph about the disadvantages. [10]

Study the two sets of answers to the examination-style reading tasks. Use the examiner's comments to help you assess and improve your own reading skills.

Student A FAIL ✗

1 Summarise the benefits of Wii Fit as described in the web page.

> This is not a benefit – it is a description.

> Why is this a benefit?

- You can go jogging
- Get a Wii Fit age score
- Have fun and get healthy
- Get an overview of your fitness

> Sensible benefits listed here.

Examiner summary

The layout is not as asked for in the question – it should be a summary not a list. The student has not picked out their ideas in the order that they appear in the article so they miss out valuable points. Close reading to highlight relevant points would have helped them. They did not read the key words in the question – it asked for benefits, not just features. They did, however, make three relevant points.

2 What different physical activities can you try on a Wii Fit? Give your answer as a list of bullet points.

> The text states rhythm boxing so this is not fully correct.

- Jogging
- Boxing
- Step aerobics
- Snowboarding
- Yoga poses

Examiner summary

The student has used the format as specified in the question, and listed five points for the five marks available. Failing to write 'rhythm' boxing costs a mark as the answer is not fully correct. As they did not locate the information in the correct order, they have missed out valuable information. They should practise close reading and highlighting to avoid this in future.

3 What is the purpose of this Wii Fit web page? Give reasons to support your answer.

> Not clear – what is 'it'?

> Vague

✗ It starts by telling you what a Wii Fit is and what you do on it so it wants to give you info about it. It wants you to buy a Wii Fit so it is trying to persuade you to buy one. It does this by telling you all of the good things ✗ and the benefits that come by using the Wii Fit.

Examiner summary

This answer begins poorly – the ideas are not linked to the question. The student spots that the text gives information, but the explanation is unclear. They realise the text is trying to persuade and give a brief explanation of 'how' but fail to mention examples of persuasive language. The answer is short and vague. To improve, the student needs to use the key word 'purpose' from the question, and mention how effective the text has been in achieving its purpose.

4 Using the first two paragraphs of the article, describe how Stuart Horsfield feels about Nintendo gaming. Make sure you use evidence to support your ideas.

Relevant points backed up with reasons.

Good use of keywords from the question.

I think that Stuart ✓ feels that gaming is a waste of time and that it could be dangerous for people to use gaming machines. He also feels that gaming is not great but that kids "love" it. ✓ He feels that gaming is bad because it is taking over old fashioned outside exercise. ✗ He feels that it is an unhealthy thing to do in your spare time as it causes children to lose sleep.

Irrelevant – not from the first two paragraphs.

Examiner summary

This answer is more focused on the question and uses the key words. The feelings are valid and reasons are given for most of these. The last sentence is not taken from the first two paragraphs so it does not gain any marks.

5 In the article, how does Stuart Horsfield make it clear that he thinks gaming is dangerous? Use the following headings in your response:
- Social issues
- Health issues
- Other dangers

Clear link to question made only here.

He thinks that the machines are not safe ✗ because lots of people have had injuries because of them. Stuart also thinks that gaming is dangerous because it causes people to miss out on sleep. He also thinks that it can damage eyes, which is also dangerous. It is also dangerous because people are not being healthy by missing out on fresh air. Another dangerous bit is that it causes problems in schools as kids don't do enough sport anyway. It is dangerous because one person got a really bad hand wound.

Examiner summary

This answer links to the question, but does not approach the article in order, so misses a number of points. The student does not lose any marks for not using the suggested headings, but a better organised answer might have gained more marks.

6 Your friend is thinking of buying a Nintendo Wii. Use the three resource materials to compile an information sheet on the advantages and disadvantages of buying a Wii.
Write a paragraph about the advantages and a paragraph about the disadvantages. [10]

Correctly grouped into advantages and disadvantages.

✓ Advantages: a Wii is a great idea for you to buy because you will be able to get fit without leaving the house and can have lots of fun doing at least 40 different exercises. The Wii is really easy to set up and is quite cheap compared to other gaming consoles. ✗
✓ Disadvantages: it might stop you from going out with your friends because you will get addicted to gaming. It stops you going outside for fresh air and it can cause you sore eyes. Some people think it's like real life so they get a bit obsessed and violent after using it.

There are ten marks, so ten points need to be made. The first paragraph includes five points but the last two points are not from the resources.

Examiner summary

The student should be looking for ten points: five advantages and five disadvantages. The last two advantages are not from the article so gain no marks. The student uses their own words to describe the disadvantages; this is fine as the points are correct and the tone of writing is appropriate, but overall this student has failed to achieve a Level 2 pass.

Student B PASS ✓

1 Summarise the benefits of Wii Fit as described in the web page.

> Key word from task.

The benefits ✓ of the Wii Fit are that you will have fun while you are using one. You can burn calories and improve your balance and posture. You can track your progress so you know when you are improving. Another benefit is that you can try out a range of different exercises.

> Benefits included in correct format – summary.

Examiner summary

The student uses the key word 'benefits' from the question. They have gone through the article in order so their answer is well organised. They have included five benefits and used the right format – a summary.

2 What different physical activities can you try on a Wii Fit? Give your answer as a list of bullet points.

- Aerobic exercises
- Muscle workouts
- Yoga poses
- Snowboarding
- Rhythm boxing

> Correct words copied from the text and bullet points used.

> Five answers to gain the five marks stated.

Examiner summary

This answer tracks the text in order, selects the correct information and copies the phrases accurately from the text. It is set out correctly using bullet points.

3 What is the purpose of this Wii Fit web page? Give reasons to support your answer.

The purpose of the web page is to tell you that a Nintendo Wii Fit is a video console with a difference as you monitor your fitness on it. When we read the rest of the article, we realise that the purpose is to give us information about the Wii Fit as it tells you how to use it and how you will benefit, "optimise your physique". Finally, I think the purpose of the web page is to persuade people to buy one because it tells you that you will have "fun" using it.

> Good references to the question.

Examiner summary

There could be a little more explanation, but the answer is detailed and focused with some strong references to the question.

4 Using the first two paragraphs of the article, describe how Stuart Horsfield feels about Nintendo gaming. Make sure you use evidence to support your ideas.

> Direct quotations to back up points.

> Reference to the question.

✓ Stuart feels that Nintendo gaming is like a fever that has ✓ "gripped the UK" so it is clear that he dislikes gaming. He also feels that gaming is replacing exercise and other stuff that is good for us so he feels that it is a nuisance. Stuart feels that kids "love" it but he can't understand why as he feels that it is causing problems.

> Another point needed – five marks are available.

Examiner summary

The student focuses on the feelings of 'Stuart' as requested, and uses quotes to back up their points. They could be more specific about the activities being lost due to the use of the Wii.

5 In the article, how does Stuart Horsfield make it clear that he thinks gaming is dangerous?
Use the following headings in your response:
- Social issues
- Health issues
- Other dangers

✓ <u>Social issues</u> Stuart thinks that gaming is dangerous because people are not exercising with friends or going out very much – for example, to the park. He also thinks that people are not talking to each other and that "quality communication" is being lost – which he feels is a shame.

✓ <u>Health issues</u> Stuart thinks that gaming is dangerous because children are having more colds and headaches and are suffering from eye strain after using games consoles. He also thinks they are dangerous because many people have suffered from physical injuries like whiplash, sprained ankles and neck injuries.

> Correct use of two of the headings taken from the question, but the third one is missing.

Examiner summary

The student picks out areas that are dangerous and the answer is well structured and organised, but needs more explanation and more coverage of the text.

6 Your friend is thinking of buying a Nintendo Wii. Use the three resource materials to compile an information sheet on the advantages and disadvantages of buying a Wii.

Write a paragraph about the advantages and a paragraph about the disadvantages. [10]

✓ <u>Advantages:</u> a Nintendo Wii can be a lot of fun and can help to give or improve your healthy lifestyle. It makes exercise varied and interesting so it makes you more interested in working out. When you are using a Wii you can get an overview of your fitness which will help you track your improvements.

> Clearly links to the question.

✓ <u>Disadvantages:</u> some people think that the Nintendo Wii stops you from socialising and can also stop people from going outside. It can also cause a number of mental and physical illnesses (like anxiety and eye strain), which is not good for you with your asthma problems. The Wii can cause you to sleep poorly especially if you are playing late at night so be careful! The Wii can cause physical injuries if not used properly (some people have had swollen eyes and even neck injuries).

> Clear organisation – headings taken from the question.

Examiner summary

A full answer clearly combining information from all three resources. Personal pieces of information make it realistic.

Speaking, listening and communication

Introduction

As part of the Functional Skills English assessment you will be tested on your skills in speaking, listening and communication. You must be able to contribute to discussions and make effective presentations. You will not be asked to 'act', but you must be able to take different roles in discussions such as chairperson, speaking, responding, and so on.

You will be given tasks and some information on which to base your responses. For discussions, you might be asked to work with unfamiliar people, such as an interviewer from the world of work, or in an unfamiliar context.

How to use the Speaking, listening and communication section of this book

The Speaking, listening and communication section takes you through the skills you need to contribute to discussions and make presentations. You can apply what you learn to any subject or context. There are eight pages of teaching and activities, to build the skills you need for effective speaking, listening and communication.

Read the learning objectives carefully to be clear what your aims are, and use the examiner tips for hints on how to pass Level 2. Use them to assess your learning to help you work towards Level 2.

At the end of the section, you will find two practice Speaking, listening and communication tasks to help you practise using your skills. You will be helped to work out what you have done well and what you need to improve on in your own work. For more information on how you will be assessed, see pages 112–15.

ACTIVITY

1 Discuss the assessment criteria.
2 Produce a list of bullet points called 'To pass Level 2 I need to …'. List the most important points you will need to remember in your Speaking, listening and communication assessments.
3 Decide which areas you are weakest in, and make sure you focus on improving your skills in these areas.

Assessment criteria

The table below lists and explains the criteria against which your speaking, listening and communication skills will be assessed. It directs you to the pages in this book that teach and practise each skill.

Make a range of contributions to discussions in a range of contexts, including those that are unfamiliar, and make effective presentations.		
Consider complex information and give a relevant, cogent response in appropriate language	This means you must be able to listen actively to information, asking questions if necessary, and use what you have heard in your own responses. You must be able to judge the relevance of the information you are given. Cogent means your responses should be reasonable, thought out and sensible.	**See pages 42/43**
Present information and ideas clearly and persuasively to others	This means you must present clearly, using notes or a well-structured plan. You should use persuasive techniques when necessary. You must be able to ask and answer questions.	**See pages 44/45**
Adapt contributions to suit audience, purpose and situation	This means listening carefully and responding to other people's views, perhaps by adapting your own. You must be aware of your audience (who you are talking to), purpose (the aim of your presentation or discussion) and situation (the context). You should adapt your language and tone and use the right level of formality.	**See pages 46/47**
Make significant contributions to discussions, taking a range of roles and helping to move discussion forward	This means you should have plenty of ideas to contribute, and be prepared to talk in detail and develop your ideas. You might be asked to lead a discussion, or contribute by listening, speaking, questioning, and so on. You should help to move the discussion forward with questions, feedback or by summarising.	**See pages 48/49**
All Speaking, listening and communication standards	Practice Speaking, listening and communication tasks and sample student answers.	**See pages 50/51**

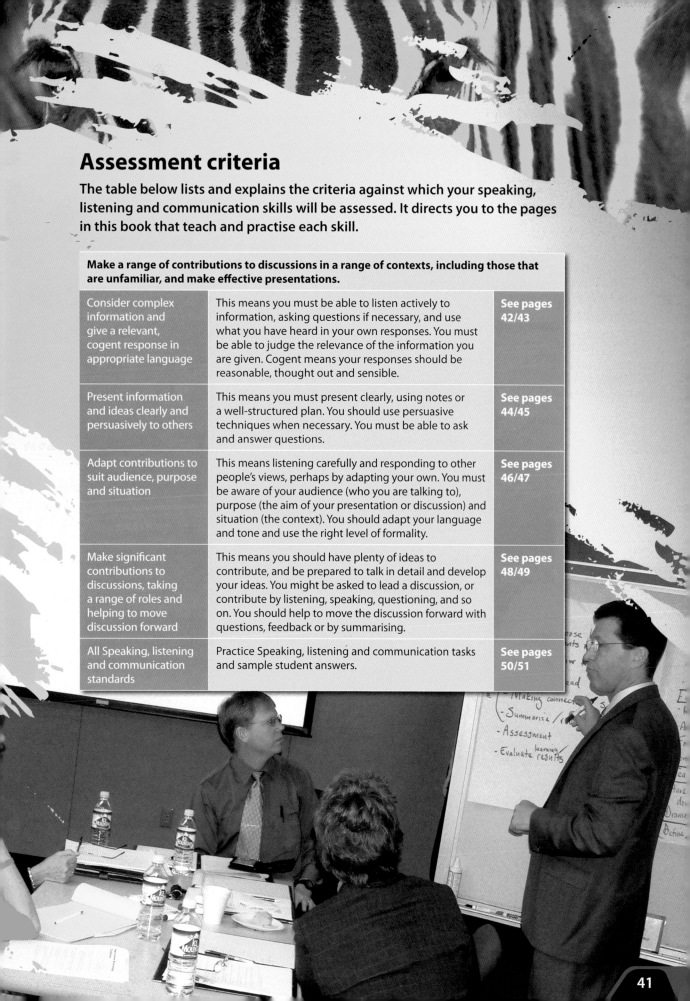

TASK: To prepare for and give a Functional Skills English assessment-style presentation about a device for monitoring young people's driving.

Active listening

Active listening is listening carefully, asking questions to make sure you have understood, and responding appropriately.

Tips for active listening

- Note key facts as you hear them.
- Make your notes brief so that you can keep listening.
- Do not interrupt.
- Ask questions at the end if there is anything you missed.
- Look at the speaker when possible to help you follow what they are saying.

ACTIVITY 1

In small groups, take turns to read aloud all or part of the newspaper article on the page opposite. Those not reading should listen actively – check the tips on how to do this.

Identifying information

When making a presentation, you must decide what information is relevant and important.

ACTIVITY 2

1 Decide on your viewpoint for the task: will your presentation be in support of the device, or make a case against it? Note it down.
2 In pairs, take it in turns to read the article out loud again. When it is your turn to listen, make brief notes on:
   - key facts about the device that should be included in your presentation
   - any points that back up your viewpoint that you could include.
3 Ask questions if you are not sure about any key points. Use the answers to add extra details to your notes.

Spy-under-the-bonnet sneaks to mum and dad when young drivers take risks

By **Ben Webster**

Parents are monitoring their teenage children's driving with a spy-under-the-bonnet device that records any dangerous manoeuvre.

If a young driver brakes or accelerates aggressively, takes a corner too fast, or pulls out suddenly to overtake, the device registers the incident and transmits the information back to the parent via the web.

The parent can log on and look at their child's safety score for each trip within 20 minutes of its completion. They can check what mistakes are being made, and when the car exceeds 70 mph.

Young drivers receive a 25 per cent discount on their insurance premium for agreeing to have the device fitted. The average teenage male driver, who pays £2,000 for third party insurance, would save £500. Participants are rewarded with shopping vouchers for each month of safe driving.

A six-month trial by Staffordshire County Council involving 40 young drivers found that the number of high-risk manoeuvres fell by 58 per cent after information from the device was fed back to parents. Fuel consumption fell by an average 10 per cent.

More than 14 young drivers and their passengers are killed every week. Men aged 17 to 20 are almost ten times more likely to be killed or seriously injured behind the wheel than those aged 40 to 59.

The system includes a dashboard unit containing green, yellow and red lights to give drivers instant feedback on their risk level. If a driver commits three high-risk manoeuvres within 10 minutes, the unit will show red for at least 20 minutes.

To make the system more acceptable to young drivers, it does not tell parents where they are driving.

Andrew Howard, head of road safety at the AA, said: 'Young drivers know how to drive safely, it's just that they choose not to. With a parent keeping an eye on them, they are less likely to show off.'

My learning objectives ▼

- To give a presentation that others can hear clearly and understand
- To persuade the audience to agree with my point of view
- To respond sensibly to points raised by the audience

Presenting information and ideas

TASK: Remind yourself of the task on page 42 before working through these pages.

Organise your ideas

Your presentation on the spy device should be organised clearly so that the audience can understand it. Remember, your aim is to:

- present information and ideas
- persuade others to agree with your viewpoint.

ACTIVITY 1

Look back at your notes from Activity 2 on page 42.

1 List key information and ideas about the spy device, including:
  - an introduction to what it is
  - how it works
  - ways in which it is a good OR a bad thing
  - facts and figures.
2 List points that might persuade others to support your viewpoint, including:
  - why *you* think it is a good or a bad thing
  - facts and figures that support your view
  - the views of others who agree with you.

Think about language

Think about the language you could use to make your presentation persuasive and clear. Use language to increase the impact of your points. For example, saying 'Tragic loss of life could be avoided by use of this device' might be more persuasive than 'This device can help to keep people safe'. You can also use words like 'first', 'however' or 'finally' to help to structure your presentation.

You can use the views of others to support your point of view

ACTIVITY 2

1 Review your points to see where you might use language for effect.
2 Read the sentence openers below. You could try using them to introduce your points. Practise saying them out loud, adding your own facts or viewpoints to complete them.

Remember to:
- make sure you can be heard
- organise relevant information and ideas clearly
- express your point of view persuasively
- try to include answers to these questions:
  What?
  Who?
  Why?
  Where?
  When?
  How?
- respond to questions politely and informatively.

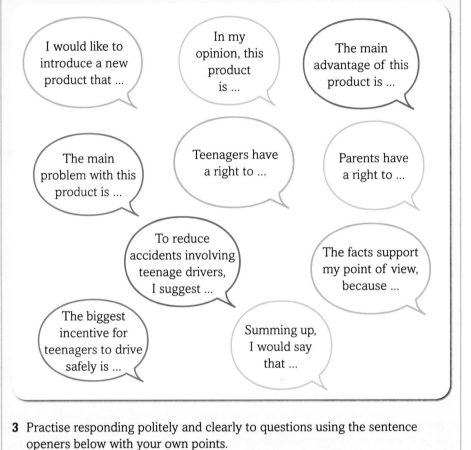

I would like to introduce a new product that …

In my opinion, this product is …

The main advantage of this product is …

The main problem with this product is …

Teenagers have a right to …

Parents have a right to …

To reduce accidents involving teenage drivers, I suggest …

The facts support my point of view, because …

The biggest incentive for teenagers to drive safely is …

Summing up, I would say that …

3 Practise responding politely and clearly to questions using the sentence openers below with your own points.

I understand your point of view. However, I feel that …

I can clarify that point by saying …

I disagree, because …

Give your presentation

Take it in turn to make your presentations. Each presentation should be about two to three minutes long. Use your notes and the tips for presenting to help you. When listening to others' presentations, prepare to ask questions and challenge ideas you disagree with.

Peer/Self-assessment

Ask for feedback from the group on your presentation and your active listening skills. What do you still need to improve to achieve Level 2?

My learning objectives ▼

- To adapt the way I talk to the audience, purpose and situation of the discussion
- To speak in appropriate language with the right level of formality

Adapting my contributions

TASK: To discuss the idea of living at home while at college or in a first job, adapting the points you make and the language you use to the audience, situation and purpose.

Peer/Self-assessment

Look at the learning objectives. Think about what you can do confidently, and what you still need to learn or practise to achieve Level 2.

Adapting contributions

'Adapting contributions' in discussions means making relevant points using just the right choice of words. How you adapt what you say and how you say it will depend on the **audience**, **purpose** and **situation** of the discussion.

KEY TERMS

The **audience** is who you are speaking to, e.g. a group of friends, or a member of staff.

The **purpose** is your reason for speaking, e.g. to explain information, or persuade your audience to agree with you.

The **situation** is where you are speaking, e.g. informally in a cafe, or formally in an interview.

ACTIVITY 1

1 Read the article on the next page.
2 Start to plan for a discussion on this issue *with your group*. Decide your viewpoint. Jot down points that would be relevant for this audience and purpose.

These ideas from the article might help you:

household chores   getting on well with family members   space and time to study

transport   privacy   security   seeing friends

contributing to the house   saving money   going out   independence

3 Now think about discussing this issue *with a member of the college staff* to explain why living at home will be good for your studies. Write down your ideas, using the article to help you.

The right choice of words

Discussions with friends are usually informal. Your tone could be chatty and you may use slang words. A discussion with a member of college staff would be formal. You should speak clearly and correctly. In all discussions, you must be polite.

ACTIVITY 2

Choose two points that you would make in each discussion. Jot down some words and phrases you might use. Make sure they are appropriate to your audience, purpose and situation.

PASS LEVEL 2 ✓

Make sure you:
- match the points you make to your audience, purpose and situation
- use appropriate language with the right level of formality.

Have your discussion

Discuss the issue of living at home while working or at college. Follow the steps in Activity 3.

Living at home (extract from *A Guide to Uni Life* by Lucy Tobin)

Unless living at home involves a transatlantic commute (obviously that sounds ridiculous, but someone I knew at uni literally did commute from New York to Oxford...) living at home will usually be the cheapest accommodation option. And there are benefits. It's free, unless your parents want a contribution towards rent, food or bills – and even if they do, it'll probably still be cheaper. There will be home-cooked meals on the table when you come home from your long day in the library, or your long night out clubbing, as it may be. And the washing machine will probably be a lot nearer your room.

But there are downsides, too. You'll probably feel a bit left out when all your uni friends are getting ready for a night out together, or bonding over mutual whinges about the lack of hot water in their halls. Unless one of your parents happens to be the university dean and you live on campus, it'll probably be a longer commute into lectures and it'll be harder to go out at night if you're living at home. There'll be higher transport costs for things like taxis, too.

If you do choose – or are financially compelled – to live at home, try to agree some ground rules with your parents to ease the situation. Tell them that you'll be considerate about coming in late, and ask them to not set a curfew. Ask them to treat you differently from the days when dad picked you up from the school disco in year 7.

You might face the problem that, to you, sitting at the desk all day reading is working, but to them it's what they do when they finish work, and they'll try to fill your day with babysitting and so on. So ensure that your parents know to leave you to study and don't ask you to do errands while you're studying. Friends who lived at home during uni tell me this kind of agreement is easier if you offer to do chores when you're not studying....

As for socialising, keep your ear to the ground about any events, be an active user of social network sites like Facebook and MySpace and the Students' Union site, ask friends to remember to keep you in the loop, and keep up with your 'home' friends too.

ACTIVITY 3

1 Decide which audience, purpose and situation you will be in.
2 Make your contributions, remembering to use appropriate language.
3 After each discussion, feed back to each other. Consider these points:
  • Were the points made relevant to the situation, purpose and audience?
  • Were the points made in appropriate language?

Peer/Self-assessment

Ask for feedback from the group on your contributions to the discussion. What do you still need to improve to achieve Level 2?

Making discussions work

TASK: To take an active part in a Functional Skills English assessment-style discussion:
Discuss the problems and benefits of technology aimed at controlling the behaviour of teenagers.

Work through the Activity to prepare your ideas for the discussion.

ACTIVITY

1 Read the texts on the next page.
2 Consider the arguments for and against the use of the Mosquito device and decide on your viewpoint.
3 Jot down some key points and ideas that support your opinion.

Taking a range of roles

During a discussion, you should aim to take a range of roles, including:

- acting as chairperson – stating the subject and purpose of the discussion, and keeping it on track
- putting forward a viewpoint
- listening carefully to other people's points and ideas
- adding to someone else's point
- questioning what someone has said
- helping others to have their say
- helping to summarise the group's views.

Moving discussions forward

Helping to move a discussion forward involves listening carefully to others and responding positively and politely. You can agree with someone and build on their points and ideas, or disagree with them and explain why. You might also move the discussion forward by adding new points and ideas for others to think about, or by inviting ideas from someone who has not yet spoken.

Have your discussion

Work in groups. Decide who will act as chairperson in each group. Discuss the group members' views about technology like the Mosquito, using your notes to get across your viewpoint.

You must show that you can play a full range of roles in a discussion. Most people are happier in one role than others – perhaps you would rather listen than speak out. Make sure you don't get 'stuck' in a single role.

The Mosquito

The Mosquito ultrasonic deterrent is the solution to the eternal problem of unwanted gatherings of youths and teenagers in shopping centres, around shops, your home and anywhere they are causing problems. The presence of these teenagers discourages genuine shoppers and customers from coming into your shop, affecting your turnover and profits. It also affects your home life if you are worrying about your retail property when you are not at work. Anti-social behaviour has become the biggest threat to private property over the last decade and there has been no effective deterrent until now.

The Mosquito is a revolutionary new device that has been specifically designed to disperse groups of teenagers from loitering in areas where they are not wanted.

| Home | About | Join | Take Action | News & Events | Issues | Publications | Contact |

You are here: **Issues**

Torture
Terrorism
Privacy
Asylum
Equality
Free Speech & Protest
ASBOs
Extradition
Human Rights Act
Young People's Rights
  Human Rights and the Mosquito
  Stamp Out The Mosquito
  Curfews

HELP US STAMP OUT THE MOSQUITO

What is the Mosquito?

Using technology originally designed to scare away vermin, the 'Mosquito' is a device that emits a very high frequency buzzing sound which cannot be heard by people over the age of 25.

This degrading and discriminatory device is now being used to deter young people from going to particular areas, with a sound that is described as 'distressing' and 'unbearable'. In 2009, there were estimated to be 3,500 such ultra-sonic dispersal devices in use across the country.

Why is the Mosquito a problem?

We are concerned that:

- The device will affect all young people, not target those who are misbehaving.
- It targets only young people when problems may also be caused by adults.
- It exposes young people to extreme discomfort as if they were worth no more than a garden pest.

This is not a proportionate response to loiterers and could adversely affect young people. We believe that the Mosquito does not encourage young people to act responsibly. Instead it simply presumes they will not.

Shami Chakrabarti, the Director of Liberty, said: 'What type of society uses a low-level sonic weapon on its children? Imagine the outcry if a device was introduced that caused blanket discomfort to people of one race or gender, rather than to our kids.

The Mosquito has no place in a country that values its children and seeks to instil dignity and respect.'

Peer/Self-assessment

Ask for feedback from the group on your contributions to the discussion. What do you still need to improve to achieve Level 2?

Plan a presentation

Read the task below and use the annotations to help you to understand what you are being asked to do.

TASK 1

Situation – part of a week of whole-school events. Your contribution needs to be well thought out, clear and persuasive.

This is your audience: use formal language, and include interesting points to keep their attention.

Use the ideas to help you. Make sure you have enough material.

Your school is planning a week of 'healthy living' events. Prepare for and give a presentation to your school's staff, governors and students about the importance of healthy living. Your aim is to persuade your audience to improve their own lifestyles. You could include points about diet, exercise, sleep and relaxation, a healthy environment, etc.

Prepare enough material to give a two-to-three-minute presentation.

Your purpose is to persuade. You need to use persuasive language.

You can come up with your own ideas, too.

Work on language

Work out some formal sentence openers to help you structure your presentation. Practise saying them aloud and including your own ideas.

My presentation today will …

Another key point is …

To encourage people to adopt a healthier lifestyle, I suggest …

Summing up, …

The most important point to consider is …

The biggest incentive for me to adopt a healthy lifestyle is …

PASS LEVEL 2 PASS LEVEL 2

Use the notes and tips on these pages to prepare for, take part in, and evaluate the practice Speaking, listening and communication tasks.

Make brief notes on the key ideas you want to include. Organise them logically and plan for an introduction and a conclusion. Refer to your notes during your presentation to make sure you stay focused and do not miss anything out.

Make notes of vocabulary that you might use, such as:

> diet   fitness   stamina   stress   calories   muscle tone   lifestyle
> consequences   energy   health   obesity   well-being   rest
> exhaustion   enthusiasm   nutrition   balanced   pollution   physical
> vitamins and minerals   mental   achieve   long-term   work-life balance

Remind yourself of some persuasive techniques, and use them.

Give your presentation

Practice giving your presentation. Make sure you:

- look at the audience whenever possible
- use your notes to help you stay focused and make your points clearly
- use formal language
- remember your purpose is to persuade
- ask for any questions at the end, and respond carefully and thoughtfully to them.

Plan for a discussion

Read the annotations below to help you understand what the task is asking you to do.

TASK 2

> Situation – part of the healthy living week, so your contribution needs to be formal and focused.

> You will be discussing with fellow students so your language can be informal.

As part of your school's 'healthy living week', you will be taking part in a discussion with fellow students on the subject:

'Are young people today screen-obsessed, unhealthy couch potatoes?'

> You will take part in a discussion. This can involve two or more people. Make sure you consider different points of view and decide on your own opinion. Make sure you can back it up with evidence.

> Prepare at least three main points on this question.

Have your discussion

Practise having the discussion. Make sure you:

- decide on a person to chair the meeting
- speak clearly, and listen carefully when others are speaking
- use your notes to help you stay focused and make your points clearly
- take a range of roles, including speaking, listening, responding, questioning, inviting others to speak.

Peer/Self-assessment

Evaluate each other's performance in each task, stating three things that were done well and one thing that could be improved.

Writing

Introduction

As part of your Functional Skills English assessment you will be tested on your skills in writing the kinds of texts that are used in everyday life. You must be able to present your ideas and information clearly and persuasively; use a range of styles; and write with few or no mistakes. You might be asked to write reports, formal or informal letters, forms and applications, leaflets, speeches, or other kinds of informative and persuasive texts.

You will be given information on which to base your answer, and will be told what kind of writing you should produce, and for whom you are writing. In all your writing, you must be able to use the correct format, write appropriately for your audience and purpose, and use the right tone.

How to use the Writing section of this book

The Writing section takes you through the skills you need to write reports, formal letters, informal letters, forms and applications, leaflets and speeches. You can apply what you learn to writing any kind of information text.

For each type of text, there are four pages of teaching and activities, to build the skills you need for writing. It is essential for your Functional Skills English assessment that your sentences, punctuation and spelling are correct, so each section also contains a page called 'Improve your accuracy'.

Read the learning objectives carefully to be clear what your aims are, and use the examiner tips for hints on how to pass Level 2. Use them to assess your learning to help you work towards Level 2.

At the end of each section, you will find two practice examination-style Writing tasks to help you practise using your writing skills. There are also two sample student answers, with comments from the examiner, to help you work out what you have done well and what you need to improve on in your own work. For more information on how you will be assessed, see pages 116–23.

ACTIVITY

1 Discuss the assessment criteria.
2 Produce a list of bullet points called 'To pass Level 2 I need to …'. List the most important points you will need to remember in your Writing assessment.
3 Decide which areas you are weakest in, and make sure you focus on improving your skills in these areas.

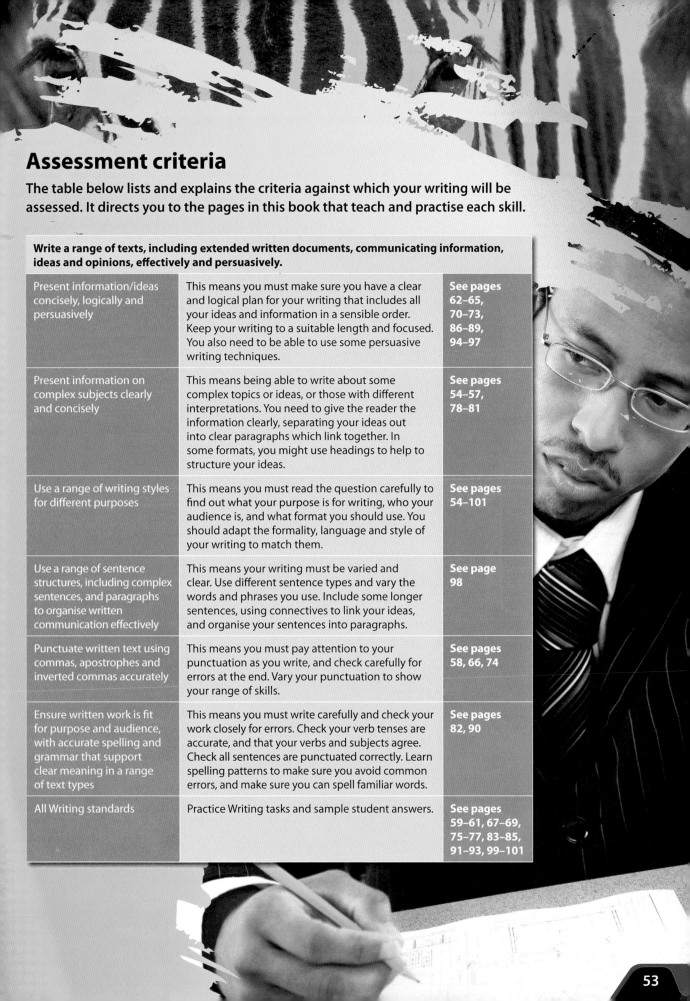

Assessment criteria

The table below lists and explains the criteria against which your writing will be assessed. It directs you to the pages in this book that teach and practise each skill.

Write a range of texts, including extended written documents, communicating information, ideas and opinions, effectively and persuasively.		
Present information/ideas concisely, logically and persuasively	This means you must make sure you have a clear and logical plan for your writing that includes all your ideas and information in a sensible order. Keep your writing to a suitable length and focused. You also need to be able to use some persuasive writing techniques.	**See pages 62–65, 70–73, 86–89, 94–97**
Present information on complex subjects clearly and concisely	This means being able to write about some complex topics or ideas, or those with different interpretations. You need to give the reader the information clearly, separating your ideas out into clear paragraphs which link together. In some formats, you might use headings to help to structure your ideas.	**See pages 54–57, 78–81**
Use a range of writing styles for different purposes	This means you must read the question carefully to find out what your purpose is for writing, who your audience is, and what format you should use. You should adapt the formality, language and style of your writing to match them.	**See pages 54–101**
Use a range of sentence structures, including complex sentences, and paragraphs to organise written communication effectively	This means your writing must be varied and clear. Use different sentence types and vary the words and phrases you use. Include some longer sentences, using connectives to link your ideas, and organise your sentences into paragraphs.	**See page 98**
Punctuate written text using commas, apostrophes and inverted commas accurately	This means you must pay attention to your punctuation as you write, and check carefully for errors at the end. Vary your punctuation to show your range of skills.	**See pages 58, 66, 74**
Ensure written work is fit for purpose and audience, with accurate spelling and grammar that support clear meaning in a range of text types	This means you must write carefully and check your work closely for errors. Check your verb tenses are accurate, and that your verbs and subjects agree. Check all sentences are punctuated correctly. Learn spelling patterns to make sure you avoid common errors, and make sure you can spell familiar words.	**See pages 82, 90**
All Writing standards	Practice Writing tasks and sample student answers.	**See pages 59–61, 67–69, 75–77, 83–85, 91–93, 99–101**

TASK: To write an answer to this Functional Skills English exam-style question: Your school's headteacher and governors have decided to review the school uniform. You have been asked to write a report for them, giving the views of your year group on school uniform. You should include information on what your year group likes and dislikes about the current uniform, and any changes that they think should be made.

Real-life reports

Reports need to be clear and accurate. Here are two examples of real-life reports.

- A surveyor reports to an architect about whether a site is safe to build houses on.
- A doctor reports to a team manager on whether a footballer is fit to play in an important match.

ACTIVITY 1

1 What is the purpose of each report above? Discuss what might happen if these reports were unclear or misleading.
2 Read the task again carefully, then read the purposes for writing below. Decide which student has understood the purpose of the task correctly.

My purpose is to state what the uniform is.

My purpose is to report to the headteacher and governors on my year's views about uniform.

My purpose is to redesign the school uniform.

3 Write the correct purpose out in your own words.

Format

To be clear, a report must be in the right **format**. A plan for the report in this task is given below. Look at it carefully and then complete Activity 2.

What the report is about, who it is for and who wrote it.

What the report is for and how the information has been gathered.

Headings and lists can divide up the information clearly.

Summary and recommendations (what should happen next)

The writer's name and position.

Heading

Introduction

Our views on school uniform
1 Paragraph on what is liked
2 Paragraph on what is not liked
Our views on possible changes
3 Paragraph on suggestions for change

Conclusion

Sign off

ACTIVITY 2

Copy out the plan above, leaving spaces to add your own notes.

Gathering and organising your information

You now need to:

- put together some information for your report
- organise the information in your plan so that your report will be clear and easy to follow.

ACTIVITY 3

1 Decide on:
- three things you like about your school uniform
- three things you do not like about your school uniform
- three changes you think should be made to your uniform.

2 Jot down your ideas in the right places on your plan.

You can use **topic sentences** to help the reader follow your writing.

ACTIVITY 4

The openings of some topic sentences are listed below.

Students think they should be able to...

Uniform is a good idea because...

The Student Council would like to suggest that...

Some students think that...

However, other students feel that...

To gain the views of the Year 10 students, I...

In conclusion, most students think that...

On your plan, write a topic sentence for each section. You could use the ideas above, or your own ideas.

My learning objectives ▼

- To make sure my writing is appropriate for the audience
- To back up my points with reasons
- To use appropriate language
- To write a clear, concise and accurate report

Get the language right

Remind yourself of the task on page 54 before working through these pages.

Audience

Always make sure you are clear about the audience for your writing. For this task, the audience is the headteacher and governors of your school. Imagine them actually reading your report. This will help you to decide what they need to know.

PASS LEVEL 2

You must adapt your writing to suit your audience. Keeping a real audience in mind can help you to do this.

ACTIVITY 1

1 Read the extracts below. Decide whether each student has thought carefully enough about the audience for this task.

Our school uniform consists of a black blazer and grey skirt or trousers.

Students in Year 10 mostly like having a school uniform though we feel that it needs to be adapted for the 21st century student.

We believe that girls should be allowed to wear trousers.

2 Now check the notes on your own plan. Have you thought carefully about what your audience needs to know and what it already knows? Make changes if you need to.

Supporting your views

In a well-written report, all the points made are supported by good reasons. The audience will not be convinced by writers who make **assertions** but cannot justify them.

ACTIVITY 2

Take another look at your plan. Make sure you can back up each point you want to make with good reasons. For example, if you stated, 'Girls should be allowed to wear trousers', you might back it up with the reason, 'because they are more practical'.

Tone

To achieve Level 2, you must match the style and tone you use to your audience and purpose. A report on a serious subject for an official audience should be written in a formal way. You should not use slang or chatty language, and you should be polite.

ACTIVITY 3

1 Look at these examples from two students' work. The first uses an appropriate tone, and the second does not. Jot down at least two things that the second student does wrong.

> We believe that the uniform needs to be changed. The colour of the sweatshirt is unpleasant and a plain black one with the school crest would be more appropriate. All the students agree that the school tie is unnecessary as it cannot be seen under the sweatshirt. An open collar white shirt would be more comfortable and practical.

> No one likes the sweatshirt! Do you really think that hideous muddy green colour makes us look good? You'd have to be blind to think it is a good look for today's young adults. No, we want something a bit livelier - maybe a choice of colours so students can decide what suits them best. This would be great!

2 Rewrite the second example using an appropriate tone. Remember to justify each point made, too.

In the examination, you are advised to spend about 30 minutes on each writing task. Practise writing to time. If you don't leave enough time to make all your points or to check your work, you could lose marks.

Review and write

You are now ready to complete the task. Write your report in full, remembering to:

- make sure you are clear about the purpose for your writing
- use the notes on your plan to make your points clearly
- help your reader to follow your writing by using topic sentences
- give reasons for your views
- use an appropriate tone
- take care with grammar, spelling and punctuation, and check your work carefully for errors when you have finished.

Peer/Self-assessment

Check your finished report. What have you done well in your writing? What needs further improvement? Make corrections to your report if you need to.

My learning objectives ▼

- To practise checking writing for accuracy
- To learn how to use apostrophes correctly

Improve your accuracy

Checking for errors

You will lose marks in the examination if your writing is not accurate. Make sure you allow yourself time to check carefully for errors in grammar, punctuation and spelling.

ACTIVITY

The paragraph below is an unchecked extract from a report.

Year 10 students views on uniform

We belive that we should change are uniform for something more stylish, the girls hate that they have to ware scirts all year specialy in winter when they is cold, they dont like having to ware ancle soxs as well. They feel that they look like babys, the boys have to ware blazors and they are akward and bulky.

Check the paragraph for errors in spelling, punctuation and grammar.
Note down each one and what type of error it is. Then write it out correctly.

Peer/Self-assessment

Look back at your finished report. How accurate is your writing? Make corrections if you need to.

Apostrophes

The first error in the paragraph above is a missing apostrophe. Apostrophes are used to show that letters or prepositions (words like of, by, for, in) have been missed out. Read the rules below on using apostrophes where a preposition has been left out (these are sometimes called 'possessive apostrophes').

RULE

An apostrophe can be used to show a preposition has been left out (and word order changed). The apostrophe goes after the last letter of the long version. This is true whether the noun is singular or plural.

Long version	Shortened version
Uniform for students.	Students' uniform.
The decision by the Governor.	The Governor's decision.
The decision by the Governors.	The Governors' decision.
A cold day in winter.	A cold winter's day.
The length of the skirt of the girl.	The length of the girl's skirt.
The length of skirts for girls.	The length of girls' skirts.
Fashion for children.	Children's fashion.
Investigate the decisions of each other.	Investigate each other's decisions.
The choice of the people.	The people's choice.
Advice for citizens.	Citizens' advice.

Exception: **it's** only refers to **it is** or **it has** (see rule on page 74).

PASS LEVEL 2

Make sure you can use both types of apostrophe correctly. See page 74 for rules on using apostrophes that replace missing letters. Remember, apostrophes indicate something is missing – make sure you do not use them in words that are just plural.

TASK 1

Your school is revising its anti-bullying policy and the headteacher is interested in students' views about this issue. You have been asked to write a report on the problem of bullying in your school, and give your ideas about how it can be stopped.

You may wish to include some of these points:

- Where and when bullying is most likely to occur.
- How effective you think the current anti-bullying policy is.
- How the existing policy could be improved.

You could also include any other aspects that you feel are important.

Write your report.

TASK 2

Your local council has decided that it needs to improve its recycling procedures. At present, households have to separate out glass, paper and plastics for recycling. The council wishes to extend this to include garden waste, cardboard and old electrical appliances.

You are a local resident and member of the community council. You support recycling, but have some concerns over the difficulties faced by households. The council has asked you to report on the issue.

Include the following points in your report, and any other points that you feel are important:

- Your views on recycling in general.
- The problems for householders of having to sort different kinds of waste material.
- Issues of access to the recycling facilities at the local tip, which has limited opening hours.
- The timing of recycling collections.
- How the council could improve recycling procedures so that garden waste, cardboard and electrical items could also be recycled.

Write your report.

In the exam, you will often be given bullet points to help you shape your answer. Sometimes you will not be given these aids but the task itself may give you an indication of the points to cover.

Student A FAIL ✗

Many errors in sentence structure, punctuation and spelling.

Tone is impolite in places and inappropriately informal throughout.

Assertion backed up with inappropriate reason – the task asks for a response to opening hours not transport.

Some attempt at report format but it is not clear that the report is on behalf of a community group.

Poor sense of audience. Tells the council what they would already know about collections.

Irrelevant information included.

Report to Bedfordshire County council about rubbish ✓

I am a householder with two children, ✗ I am fed up with the councils ✗ approach to refuse colection. ✗ I think it is rediculous ✗ what we are expected to do, ✗ I have to sort out every week all our junk into four different bags, one for paper, another for glass, another for plastic and the rest in the general waste. ✗ I am fed up with having to put all our stuff out on the right day and then find it hasn't been taken because their was a bottle top left sticking out of the bin or our bags were too heavy for our weak bin men to lift. ✗ We are told to take our electrical stuff to the tip but I haven't got a car to do this. What does the council expect me to do – hire a taxi? ✗ My two kids ✗ make a lot of rubbish with their coke cans and take away boxes. ✗ What am I supposed to do to keep the amount of rubbish down?

✓ I think it is time to go back to weekly collections when we can put our bin out with as many bags as we like, ✗

Yours truely
Maggie Brown (Mrs)

A recommendation is made, but is not properly backed up with reasons.

Inappropriate ending. It is not a letter.

Examiner summary

This student has made some fair points but some parts of the task are not attempted: cardboard and garden waste policies and the opening hours of waste facilities are not covered. The points made are not developed with appropriate reasons for the views. The sense of audience is weak. The writer tells the council things it will already know about the current policy. The tone is also poor – a chatty informal style is not appropriate for the purpose and audience of the task. There are some features of the correct format for a report, though headings and bullet points could have given the student a stronger structure. Paragraphs are not used to indicate different areas covered, and there are no topic sentences. There is no need for the 'Yours truly' at the end, and the report lacks an appropriate introduction and conclusion. This attempt would not gain a Level 2 pass for 'Content and organisation'.

There are a number of errors in the report, including comma splicing and misspellings. The sentence structures are unvaried: too many begin with 'I'. This report would not gain a Level 2 pass for 'Sentence structure, punctuation and spelling'.

Student B PASS ✓

✓ A report to Oldham Town Council from Mossley Community Council on waste disposal and recycling.

> A clear sense of audience and purpose.

✓ Introduction
The council has asked for a report on the way in which waste is collected and other recycling issues. The Community Council has considered the issues and these are its findings. ✓

> Good use of topic sentences.

✓ 1. Firstly, we are all agreed that we need to recycle as much household waste as possible and fully support the councils ✗ approaches to this issue. There are, however, a number of aspects about the current situation which we are worried about.

> Some errors in accuracy, but mostly correct.

✓ 2. Regarding the issue of the sorting of rubbish, the storage of the bags is a major problem in our area ✓ since most of the houses have no garage and many are terraced. We find that our kitchens and back yards are filling up with rubbish bags. ✓ In addition, there is a problem with the amount of waste that is collected. Refuse collectors come every other week but will not take away more than one bag of each kind of waste. As suggested above, ✓ this results in a build up of waste materials in our homes. ✓ The council should consider whether collections every other week are sufficient, especially for families with young children.

> Statements are clearly backed up with reasons.

✓ Conclusion
We believe that the council is doing its best to become more ✓ eco-friendly, but it needs to reconsider how many bags we are allowed to put out for the dustbin men, and it should arrange for home collection of some items.

Signed: Angela Thompson (Mrs)
✓ Secretary of the Mossley Community Council

> Good use of report format, with clear headings, introduction and conclusion, and correct sign off. Variety of sentence structures.

Examiner summary

This report is strong in all respects. The student wisely follows the bullet points (**N.B points 3–5 not printed above owing to lack of space**) making additional points based on her experience of living in a particular area. There is good coverage of the issues. The tone adopted is suitably formal and the student writes with clarity and a good sense of purpose. The format is correct for a report and there is a full understanding of the requirements of the task. This work would gain a Level 2 pass for 'Content and organisation'.

The student makes a couple of simple slips, but otherwise the work is accurate and fluent and would gain a pass at Level 2 for 'Sentence structure, punctuation and spelling'.

Format, audience, purpose and tone

TASK: To write an answer to this Functional Skills English exam-style question:
The council has decided to merge your school with another school three miles away. Write a letter to the council (invent a suitable address) to explain why you feel it is a bad idea to merge the schools, and to persuade the council to change its mind.

Format

A serious letter on a serious subject to an official body should be a formal letter. This means that it must be laid out in a certain way, in the correct format. The model below shows how to start and finish a formal letter.

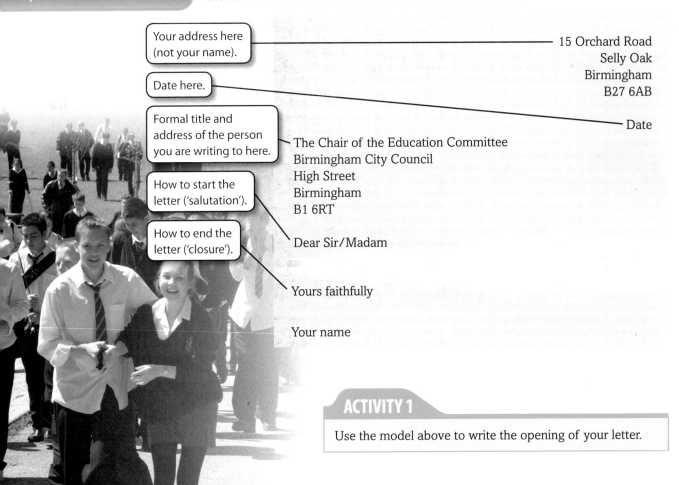

Your address here (not your name). — 15 Orchard Road / Selly Oak / Birmingham / B27 6AB

Date here. — Date

Formal title and address of the person you are writing to here. — The Chair of the Education Committee / Birmingham City Council / High Street / Birmingham / B1 6RT

How to start the letter ('salutation'). — Dear Sir/Madam

How to end the letter ('closure'). — Yours faithfully

Your name

ACTIVITY 1

Use the model above to write the opening of your letter.

Purpose

Your purpose is the reason why you are writing.

ACTIVITY 2

1 Jot down the heading 'Purpose', then read the task again. You are asked to write a letter to do what? Write the words after 'explain' under your heading.

2 To achieve your purpose, you will need to put forward at least three reasons why you oppose the merger. Think about:
   - travel
   - teaching staff
   - disruption
   - uniform
   - rivalry between the schools
   - any other points you could make.

3 Make a note of your three best ideas.

KEY TERMS

Format is the way you lay out your writing.

Purpose is the reason why you are writing.

Audience is the person, or people, you are writing to.

Tone is your style of writing and the language you use.

Audience

The audience for a letter is the person or people you are writing to.

ACTIVITY 3

Write down the heading 'Audience', then look again at the task. Who are you asked to write to? Make a note of this under your heading.

Tone

Before you start to write, think about the tone of your letter. This means the kind of language you use and the style of writing. In a business letter, the tone and style should be formal.

ACTIVITY 4

1 Which of these sentences has a formal tone?

   Don't you dare do anything to my school!

   You are a complete idiot for thinking up this stupid plan.

   While I can understand the need to economise, I do not think this is the right way of doing it.

2 Look back at the reasons why you think the merger is a bad idea. Rewrite your ideas using a formal tone. Here are some words and phrases you might wish to use:

   Firstly, I believe …

   There are a number of reasons why …

   In addition, …

   In conclusion …

PASS LEVEL 2

Make sure you understand the key terms on these pages. Pay attention to them in everything you write.

Style and organisation

TASK: Remind yourself of the task on page 62 before working through this section.

Being concise

When you are writing, you need to think about the way in which you present your views or information.

ACTIVITY 1

1 Read the two extracts below. Both are making the point that the school has been an important part of the community for many years.

Extract 1

I can't understand why you want to close my school down. It's been here a long time and it has served the community well. My Dad went to this school and he did all right. He didn't have far to walk to get here and he enjoyed his time here. Some of his teachers teach me as well and they often tease me about what my dad was like. He did well in his exams and he's done OK because he's a plumber now and he wants me to work with him when I leave school.

Extract 2

The school has served the community well for a number of generations and it deserves to stay open. If you ask the parents of the students here, they will support this point. They are all extremely grateful for what the school has offered to them and their children.

2 Which extract makes the point concisely and in an appropriate formal tone?
3 Try rewriting Extract 1 to make it more concise. You should aim to make the same points using more formal language. Leave out any information that you think is not relevant.

Organising your ideas logically

Imagine explaining how to buy a sandwich in the canteen. You would not explain that you put your change back in your pocket before saying that you should choose what you want and pay for it. All writing should follow a logical order that the audience can follow and understand.

ACTIVITY 2

1 When you were thinking about purpose, you were asked to come up with at least three points you could make against the merger. Remind yourself of your ideas.
2 Now think about a logical order for your ideas. For example, you could put first the point you feel most strongly about, or you could group ideas together such as 'Things that are good about our school', then 'Things that would be bad about the merger'. Plan to group your ideas into paragraphs.
3 Write a short list of the points you want to make, using a logical order. Make sure you have a clear beginning and end.

Using an effective style

This task does not just ask you to explain your views. It also asks you to persuade the council to change its decision. This means you have to use the kind of language that will convince the audience of the points you are making. You should also aim to use a range of sentence structures to keep the interest of your audience.

ACTIVITY 3

1 Look at the pairs of sentences. For each pair, which is the most persuasively written?

> The school is good./The school has a fantastic reputation and excellent exam results.
>
> Rival students could fight each other./Rival students could disrupt the community with distressing fights.
>
> The staff are good./The staff are well-qualified and highly thought of.

2 Go back over your list of the points you want to make. Think about how you could write them persuasively. Make notes. Remember, you still need to use a formal tone and be polite and concise.

Your spelling and punctuation must be accurate with few or no mistakes. Always check your work carefully.

Review and write

Now write your letter. Remember to pay attention to all the key points you have learnt in this unit. When you have written your letter, check it against this list to see if you are on track for a Level 2 pass.

	Yes (Pass)	Maybe	No (Fail)
Are the addresses in the right places?			
Is the date in the right place?			
Have I used the correct salutation ('Dear Sir/Madam')?			
Have I paragraphed the letter?			
Have I included four or five clear, developed points?			
Are my points logically organised?			
Is my writing concise and to the point?			
Is my tone appropriately formal?			
Have I used effective persuasive language?			
Have I used a range of sentence structures?			
Have I used the right closure ('Yours faithfully')?			
Is my punctuation accurate?			
Is my spelling accurate?			

Peer/Self-assessment

Think about what you have learnt about writing a formal letter. Write down any areas for which you scored 'Maybe' or 'No' in the checklist. You need to work on these to achieve Level 2.

My learning objectives ▼

- To learn and practise how to use commas correctly

Improve your accuracy

Commas

Many students lose marks in the examination because they do not use commas correctly. Make sure you know exactly how and when to use commas to help you achieve Level 2.

Try to memorise these rules to help you to use commas correctly. Check your work carefully to make sure you have not missed any commas, or used a comma where you need a full stop. If you use commas incorrectly in the examination, you will lose marks.

RULES

Use commas …	
To separate items within a list. Remember that the last two points in a list are joined by 'and' and do not need a comma between them.	For example: Teachers, administrative staff, governors and students all disagree with this change.
Around words like 'therefore', 'moreover' and 'however'.	For example: We think, therefore, that we should not close this school. However, we do agree that some changes are needed.
To separate a less important part of a sentence from the main part.	For example: less important part of the sentence main part of the sentence While we know that there must be changes, we are determined to keep the school open. Our caretaker, Mr Ron Brown, takes great pride in keeping the school clean.
Do not use a comma …	
In between separate sentences when you really need a full stop.	For example, the comma here should be a full stop: Most students are very happy at the school, there is a strong sense of community in the school.

'Comma splicing' – using a comma where a full stop is needed – is a common error. Check your work carefully to avoid this mistake.

ACTIVITY 1

Read the paragraph below. The student has not used commas correctly. Copy out the passage and put commas in the correct places. Remember to look out for where commas are wrongly inserted as well as where they are missing. Re-read the rules above if you are not sure.

All the people working in the school including teachers students the office staff and the caretaker would suffer if it were to close, the students would have to move to new schools find new friends and start different courses, this would be very difficult for them. Moreover the cleaning staff would be out of jobs. The Chair of Governors Mrs Jackie Phillips has said that she will fight the plan to close the school.

Peer/Self-assessment

Look back at your finished formal letter. How accurate is your writing? Make corrections if you need to.

TASK 1

Your town council is worried about the behaviour of teenagers in the town centre at night. It has proposed bringing in a curfew for young people between the ages of 11 and 16. This means that all young people will have to stay at home after 8 pm.

Write a letter to the council (inventing addresses suitable for your area) explaining why you are opposed to the proposed curfew, and persuading the council to change its mind on this issue.

You may like to include in your letter some of these points:

- A curfew is unfair because not all young people are badly behaved.
- A curfew will prevent young people from attending evening activities like football, or going to youth clubs.
- Other ways of stopping bad behaviour.
- The difficulty of enforcing a curfew because some young people look older than others.
- Other suggestions you would like to make.

Write your letter.

TASK 2

Staff at a secondary school have organised a weekend trip for Year 8 students to a local adventure centre.

The details of the trip are:

Dates and times: Leave Friday 12th June after school

Return Sunday 14th June late afternoon

Cost: Approximately £70 per student

Planned activities: Nature walks, canoeing, mountain biking, assault courses

You have been asked to write a letter from staff to parents/guardians giving details about the weekend. The letter should give all the relevant information, as well as encouraging them to send their child, and to let the school know if they wish to do so. It could also include information about clothing and spending money, and anything else you think is relevant.

Write your letter.

Read Task 2 on page 67. Then study the two examples of formal letters written by students in response to the task.

Student A FAIL ✗

Incorrect format for formal letter – sender's address in the wrong place.

Hilltop School ✗
Hilltop Lane
Derby
DE11 4SQ
Monday 11th May 2009

Dear Parents/Gardians ✗

Many spelling errors.

Little variety of sentence structure.

We are writing to you with regards to our year 8 adventure weekend. ✗ We have orginise ✗ a trip for the year 8 students to go on an adventure weekend away. The cost of this trip will cover all expenses, e.g. meals, accomodation, ✗ activitys ✗ and travel. Activitys ✗ include: Nature walks, canoeing, mountain biking and different types of assault courses. We will be leaving on Friday 12th of June (after school) and returning on Sunday 14th June late afternoon. ✗ The children are advised to bring 2 pairs of short and trousers (track suit bottoms) and three tops which they feel comfy ✗ in 2 pairs of trainers, and clean underwear and so on. ✗ The children would probably like to visit the gift shop. We advise they bring no more than £20. All together the trip costs £70 per student. ✗ More details will be sent out to those who wish to attend. ✗

Information is not presented clearly – no paragraph breaks or headings.

Language is too informal.

No persuasive writing to encourage parents/guardians to sign up.

Weak punctuation.

Yours sincerely ✗
Year 8 teachers.

Wrong closure.

Most information is included, but request to contact the school if interested is missing.

Examiner summary

The student is clear about audience. However, the letter is undeveloped and short. Most of the information is included, but not all – and the writer has given little thought to how it could be organised, divided into paragraphs, and developed to encourage parents/guardians to sign up. By giving information but not writing persuasively, the student has addressed only part of the purpose of the letter.

There are several errors in the format, which means that it has not been correctly presented as a formal letter. There are also errors in spelling and punctuation, and sentence structures show little variety, meaning the writing is not engaging.

Remember that in writing tasks you are given marks for 'Content and organisation' and 'Sentence structure, punctuation and spelling'. You need to make sure you achieve in all of these areas to pass Level 2.

Student B PASS ✓

Correct format for formal letter – sender's address in the right place; salutation correct.

Hilltop School
✓ Hilltop Lane
Derby
DE11 4SQ
11/5/09

Information presented clearly and logically with paragraph breaks for each new subject area.

Dear Parents and Guardians ✓

✓ I am delighted to say that we have arranged a weekend trip for Year 8 to a local adventure centre.

✓ The trip will take place on the weekend of 12th June till Sunday 14th June. Students will leave after school on Friday and return to school on the Sunday late afternoon. The cost of the trip is approximately £70, which should be paid as soon as possible.

Over the weekend students will be taking part in many activities such as nature walks, along rivers and hills; canoeing, which will be timed along a certain course; mountain biking in a special arena; and various assault courses testing stamina and strength of all our students. ✓ There will also be exciting surprise activities ✓ for the children.

We advise that students bring old shoes and clothes that will keep them warm, for example trainers, tracksuits and long tops, jumpers, etc. No phones, iPods or any other gadgets are needed on the trip, so please keep them at home.

We may visit local shops and towns, so students may wish to bring money to spend on souvenirs. We suggest the maximum spending money is £10. Please make sure any money is put in a named envelope ready to hand to the teacher.

If you need any further information, please do not hesitate to ring or see me. Please let me know as soon as possible if you would like to sign your child up for this fun, motivating weekend.

Yours faithfully ✓
Alex Smith
Head of Year 8

Persuasive language used to encourage parents to sign up.

Good range of sentence structures.

Accurate punctuation and spelling.

Language appropriately formal in tone.

All necessary information included.

Persuasive language used to encourage parents to sign up.

Correct closure.

Peer/Self-assessment

With a partner, create a set of rules for writing formal letters at Level 2. Use the examiner comments and tips to help you focus on what is important. You can then assess your work against these rules in future.

Examiner summary

The student is clear about audience and purpose, and the writing is both clear and persuasive. A range of sentence structures and some interesting vocabulary makes the writing engaging. The letter is well developed and organised, including relevant details in a logical order. The format is correct for a formal letter. Spelling and punctuation are accurate throughout.

Structuring and planning an informal letter

TASK: To write an answer to this Functional Skills English examination-style question:
A friend has become very keen on using Internet chat rooms. You are worried that she may be giving too much personal information on her site. Write an informal letter to your friend. You should explain that she might be putting herself at risk, and persuade her to be more careful.

Format

Informal letters are those you write on personal subjects to people you know. They have a similar **format** to a formal letter, but you do not need to include the address of the person you are writing to.

KEY TERM

The **format** is the way you lay out and structure your writing. It is not the actual content.

ACTIVITY 1

1 Look at the model formal letter on page 62 and compare it to the informal letter below.
2 How are the formats of the two letters different? Write a list of differences.

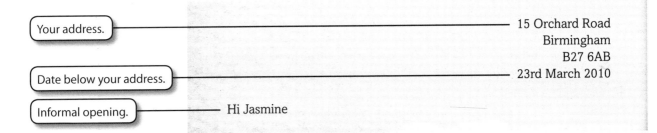

Your address.

15 Orchard Road
Birmingham
B27 6AB
23rd March 2010

Date below your address.

Informal opening.

Hi Jasmine

Informal ending, e.g. 'Love', or 'All the best'.

Love

Your first name.

Carla

Audience

Your audience is the person you are writing to. In this task, you are writing to a friend, so you already have plenty of things in common with your audience. You can include in your letter things that you both know about.

ACTIVITY 2

Decide on a friend to be your audience. Note down some things that you could refer to in your letter to them, for example about family members, school or shared interests.

If you imagine you are writing to an actual person, your letter is likely to seem more 'real'. Keep your chosen audience in mind as you write, but make sure you stay focused on the reason you are writing too.

Purpose

To write effectively, you need to be absolutely clear why you are writing – your purpose. You can then plan your writing to meet that purpose.

ACTIVITY 3

1 Read the task again carefully and start to plan your writing. Jot down as headings the two things you are asked to do in your letter (your purpose).

2 Write two or three points that you want to make under each heading. You could think about:
- the information your friend is putting on her site
- how she is handling messages from people she does not know
- the risks she is taking
- what arguments might persuade her to act differently
- the advice you would like to give her.

3 Check that you have organised your points logically under the right headings.

The examination question will give you your purpose for writing – make sure you read it carefully and note down exactly what you are asked to do.

My learning objectives ▼

- To write using an appropriate tone
- To write persuasively
- To develop my points effectively
- To write a well-structured and persuasive informal letter

Writing effectively

TASK: Remind yourself of the task on page 70 before working through this section.

Tone

You always need to match the language you use to your audience and purpose. In an informal letter to a friend, you should use a friendly, informal tone and avoid sounding critical.

ACTIVITY 1

Look at the sentences below. They are all taken from letters written in response to the task. Decide which are too formal and which have a pleasant, friendly tone. Discuss how you came to your conclusions.

> I'm really worried that you are heading for trouble using chat rooms.
>
> It has come to my attention that you are going to get into trouble with the way you are using the Internet.
>
> As your friend, I feel it is my duty to tell you that I disapprove of your actions.
>
> I'm your best friend, and we've known each other long enough for me to be straight with you.

Writing persuasively

Persuasive writing aims to make the audience agree with the writer. Some techniques for writing persuasively are:

- using emotive language
- asking questions to draw the reader in
- avoiding criticism and instead emphasising positive points.

ACTIVITY 2

Rewrite the sentences below to sound persuasive. The first one has been done for you. Try to use some of the persuasive techniques listed above.

> **1** You're taking stupid risks and I'm worried.
>
> Please can you think about the risks you're taking? I'm desperately worried for you.
>
> **2** I thought you were smart, but you've got to be more stupid than I realised.
> **3** You're asking for trouble.

Developing your arguments

If you want to persuade someone to do something, it is not enough just to use persuasive language. You must also make a good argument for your point of view. You have to give good reasons for your opinions, and develop your points.

ACTIVITY 3

Look back at the notes you made when you were thinking about the purpose of this letter. For each of the points you decided to make, try to think of at least two ways in which you could develop your argument. You could think about giving more details, using examples, and explaining exactly what you mean.

Starting and finishing your letter

You may wish to start your letter with a chatty sentence before you introduce the main reason for writing. You can finish the letter with another friendly sentence before you sign off.

ACTIVITY 4

1 Look at these two opening paragraphs for this letter. Decide which is appropriate for starting an informal letter to a friend, and why.

> I am writing to you because I am really worried about the stuff you are putting up on your chat room site. I think you need to carefully consider what you are doing and the messages you are giving out ...

> Don't fall over with surprise about getting a letter from me through the post! Believe me, there's a reason why I am putting pen to paper rather than leaving you a message on your web page ...

2 Have a go at writing a friendly closing sentence. Remember to write informally, and include some personal points.

Review and write

Now have a go at writing your letter. Make sure that you:

- use what you have learned about format to lay your letter out correctly
- write appropriately for your audience and purpose and include persuasive language
- use the notes on your plan to organise and develop your key points into paragraphs – you should have four or five developed points
- include friendly opening and closing sentences
- check your work carefully to make sure you have not made any errors in spelling, punctuation or grammar.

Peer/Self-assessment

Check your finished letter. What have you done well in your writing? What needs further improvement? Make corrections to your letter if you need to.

My learning objectives ▼

- To learn how to use full stops correctly
- To learn how to use apostrophes correctly

Improve your accuracy

Full stops

Make sure you can use full stops correctly.

> **RULE**
>
> | Use a full stop at the end of a complete sentence. | For example:
Do not put too much information on your site .
It is important to think about safety . |
> |---|---|

Apostrophes

Many students make mistakes in using apostrophes. Here is the rule for using apostrophes that replace missing letters (these are sometimes called 'apostrophes of omission').

Make sure you can use both types of apostrophe correctly. Look back to page 58 to remind yourself of the rule on using apostrophes that replace missing prepositions.

> **RULE**
>
> | Use an apostrophe when you are shortening two words into one word. The apostrophe goes above where a letter or letters have been missed out. | For example:
I am → *I'm*
He does not → *He doesn't* |
> |---|---|

> **ACTIVITY**
>
> **1** Shorten each pair of words into one word using apostrophes.
>
> | **is not** | **he is** | **they are** | **dare not** | **cannot** | **what is** | **I would** |
> |---|---|---|---|---|---|---|
>
> **2** Read this extract from a student's letter.
>
> > Im worried about how much information youre putting on your site, all that stuff about your age (which isnt true anyway) and what you like to do, I think you are giving too much away and if you arnt careful youll have lots of 'friends' who arnt friends at all but creepy men. Honestly Jasmine, you realy should think about your privacy levels, you know the provider will change them for you but youll have to give your proper age.
>
> **3** Use what you have learnt about how to use full stops and apostrophes to spot the errors in the extract.
>
> **4** Rewrite the extract correctly, and check carefully to make sure you have not missed any errors.

PASS LEVEL 2

TASK 1

One of your friends has become involved in a gang. At the moment he is not breaking the law, but you are worried about the future. His parents know nothing about it. You cannot email or text him privately, so you have decided to send him a letter explaining your concerns.

You may wish to include the following points:

- That he has many other friends he can turn to.
- That he may go to court for his involvement in the gang's activities.
- The effect of a criminal record on future college and/or job prospects.
- What his parents would say/do if they found out.
- What you think he should do.
- Any other ideas you may have.

Write your letter.

TASK 2

You have recently moved to a new area and have started at a new school. Write a letter to a friend from your old school giving your impressions of your new situation.

You may like to include the following points:

- Information about your new house and the area in general.
- How your family are settling in.
- What you think of your new school.
- Any new friends you have made so far.
- Things you miss from your old home and area.
- Anything else you feel is appropriate.

Write your letter.

PASS LEVEL 2

Study the two examples of informal letters written by students in response to the examination-style Task 2 on page 75. Use the examiner's comments to help you to assess and improve your own writing.

Student A FAIL ✗

Informal sign on and off are correct but her own address is missing, so the format is not completely correct.

✓ Dear Jane

I have now settled into my new home and school. The school is quite good but the teachers are much stricter and the lessons seem very hard, ✗ it was difficult to make new friends and I havn't ✗ got many yet though there is one girl who has been kind to me and shown me around a bit. There isnt ✗ any youth clubs around here and the place is a bit posh compared with where we used to live. ✗ I cant practice my dance routines at lunchtime in school because they dont seem to like kids doing anything like that. My brother Kyle ✗ doesnt like his primary school because hes missing his friends. Im missing you as well as there isnt any really nice people living near me who go to my school, the neighbours are old and they have allready complained to my mum about the noise of my music. Ive got a bigger bedroom though and thats nice, it has lovly pink curtains and a thick carpet, the windows look onto the street and so I can see whose ✗ about. Write soon,

Some content not relevant for the audience.

Many errors in sentence structure, punctuation and spelling.

✓ Love

Informal sign on and off are correct.

Maria xxx

Information is not organised, for example comments on friendships appear throughout the letter. Following the structure in the task could have helped.

Examiner summary

The tone of the letter is suitably friendly, but the student shows that she has not thought carefully about her audience when she includes information they would already know, such as the name of her brother and the reference to 'where we used to live'. The content is not well organised – it jumps around the different aspects that should be covered. However, the student is clear about her purpose. The letter lacks a suitable format at the beginning, and ends abruptly. It is also too short. This would not gain a Level 2 pass for 'Content and organisation'.

Punctuation errors, including comma splicing and apostrophe misuse, are common in the letter. A number of simple words are misspelt. Careful checking would have reduced the number of such errors. This would not gain a Level 2 pass for 'Sentence structure, punctuation and spelling'.

Student B PASS ✓

27 Southam Road ✓

Newcastle

NE99 2BN

29th May 2010

Correct format.

✓ Hi Jared ← Correct format.

✓ Thought I'd drop you a line and tell you how I'm getting on even though you have probably forgotten who I am by now! ✓

✓ Well, I'm here and a bit settled. It's not like being in London though and I'm missing those nights out we had at the football club. They don't understand up here that Arsenal is a much better team than Newcastle. Still, one lad I've met has promised to take me to St James Park when the Gunners come up to visit. Bit worrying, I'll be a lone voice and lucky to escape with my life if I wear my red scarf! ✓

Strong sense of audience, with appropriate tone and content.

Information is organised into paragraphs and everything in the task is covered.

✓ School's not bad. They are an OK bunch and they soon welcomed me into the Under16 team when they saw my goal-scoring skills in the lunchtime kick about! ✓ It's good to have girls around too – you don't know what you're missing going to a single-sex school! ✓ Luckily they're doing similar courses to the ones we were doing in the old school so I have fitted in quite well. ✓ Not been kicked out yet anyway, though the Head is a bit scary! ✓

Points are developed with additional information.

Strong sense of audience, with appropriate tone and content.

✓ The new house is good! Bigger than our old one and I've got a room to myself – no more listening to my brother snoring! There's plenty of space for you to come and visit. The neighbourhood is a bit quiet and there are no other kids around that I've met, but I'll soon make more friends from the football team.

Information is organised into paragraphs and everything in the task is covered.

Mum is running around like mad trying to organise us all, but Dad just sits watching the football as he always has. Julie loves school because she is in the same one as me and there are <u>boys</u>.

Time to eat. Keep in touch. Sorry to miss the game on Saturday,

✓ Cheers ← Correct format.

Sam

Examiner summary

The letter has a suitably friendly and chatty tone and the information is appropriate. There is a very good sense of engagement with the task and, by referring to shared knowledge and experiences, the writer is clearly aware of his audience. The purpose is clear and the format accurate. This would gain a pass at Level 2 for 'Content and organisation'.

There are no punctuation or spelling errors and the sentence structures are varied. This would easily gain a Level 2 pass for 'Sentence structure, punctuation and spelling'.

Peer/Self-assessment

What have you have learnt about writing an informal letter? Make notes under the headings: audience, tone, format and purpose. Is there anything you still need to improve?

My learning objectives ▼

- To understand common formats for forms and applications
- To complete forms and applications correctly for their purpose and audience
- To write clearly, logically and in the right tone

TASK: To write an answer to this Functional Skills English examination-style question: Your school bus had a collision with a car on the way home. You were slightly injured. The police want you to fill in a form giving a full and accurate account of what happened. The information you give will be used to help the police decide if further action needs to be taken against the drivers involved, and to support any insurance claims.

Peer/Self-assessment

Look at the learning objectives. Think about what you know and can do confidently, and what you still need to learn or practise to achieve Level 2.

Forms give you your format for writing. Your focus should be on selecting the right information and putting it in the right places, and making sure your writing is clear and appropriate for the purpose and audience of the form.

Real-life forms

Throughout your life, you will need to fill in various forms. For example:

- an application for a driving licence or passport
- an application for a bank account
- an insurance claim form
- a rental or mortgage agreement
- an accident report.

Your writing will need to be clear, concise and accurate so that the reader can find all the relevant information easily.

ACTIVITY 1

Choose one of the forms listed above. What might happen if your chosen form is not filled in accurately and correctly? Discuss your ideas and come up with two key reasons for learning to fill in forms correctly.

The task form

Read the outline form for the task, below.

Part A
Name:
Address:
Date of birth:

Part B
Date of incident: Time of incident:
Nature of injury:

Part C
Write below an exact account of the incident as you witnessed it, including how you became injured. Give exact details about: where the incident took place; the order of events; your location at the time of the accident; the weather conditions; anything else you believe to be relevant.

The above is a true and complete record of the accident and my injury.
Signed: Date:

Basic facts

The task form is in three parts. For Parts A and B, you are simply giving factual information. Most forms will have sections like this.

ACTIVITY 2

1 Copy out the form on a clean page, leaving spaces for the information.
2 Fill in the information required for Part A.
3 Read Part B of the form again. Make notes on what you are going to write – you will have to make up the details.
4 Fill in your information on Part B of your copy of the form.
5 Check your work for accuracy and correct any errors.

Purpose and audience

Re-read the task and Part C of the form. The purpose of filling in a form like this is to give the police a clear and honest picture of what happened, and what the consequences have been. Your writing needs to be concise – this means you should cover all the key **facts** but not include irrelevant points. Your audience – the police – want to be able to find the relevant facts quickly and easily.

ACTIVITY 3

1 Write a list of the information you need to include in Part C. Make notes on what you are going to write for every item on your list.
2 Check your notes against Part C of the form to make sure you have not missed anything.

Fact and opinion

Your audience does not need your **opinion** on the accident. It is not up to you to decide who was at fault, for example. You should just stick to the facts. Your purpose is to write what you know to be the case – not what you think might have happened.

ACTIVITY 4

1 Read what this student has written for Part C of the form. There are some facts, but there are also opinions. The student also includes some guesses about what might have happened.

As we came round the corner, I think that the stupid children at the front of the bus must have distracted the bus driver. I believe that he was looking round at them, but I didn't see this. Then there was a crash on the side of the bus and I saw one of the boys pushed across the seat by the force of the collision. After that I heard the students on the top floor shouting and screaming. I think they might have seen the car which hit us. The driver asked us all to leave the bus and stand on the pavement. I thought I heard some moans from the top floor as if someone was in pain, but I may have been mistaken.

2 Jot down the facts included by the student. Check the facts against the exact details required for Part C. Has the student missed anything out?
3 Now list the opinions and guesses included by the student. Discuss why these are not appropriate for the audience and purpose of the form.

PASS LEVEL 2

Check your own work in the same way as you checked the paragraph in Activity 4. If you spot any opinions or guesses, take them out. If you have missed out any key points that are asked for, add them in.

My learning objectives ▼

- To write in the right tone
- To complete the form, presenting my information clearly and logically

The right tone

TASK: Remind yourself of the task on page 78 before working through this section.

Tone

If you write in an inappropriate tone, your work may not be taken seriously by your audience. For example, the police would not be impressed by jokes in an accident report.

It may be useful to keep a record of the kinds of writing you practise for the examination and note for each whether the writing should be formal, informal, factual, persuasive, concise, direct, chatty, and so on. Check your record before the examination to help you remember what you have learned about tone.

ACTIVITY

Look at the list of tones below. Discuss which would be inappropriate for this task, and why. Write in your notes the three that you think would be the most appropriate for this task. Keep your purpose and audience in mind to help you make your choices.

> informal   formal   light-hearted   chatty
>   factual   exciting   friendly   rude
> emotional   persuasive   objective
>   threatening   jokey   enthusiastic

Review and write

Read through your notes for Part C and then finish the form by completing this section, using your notes. Make sure that:

- the content and tone of your work are appropriate for your purpose and audience
- you check carefully for accuracy, and correct any errors.

Application forms

- To complete an application form
- To present information accurately and persuasively

TASK: To write an answer to this Functional Skills English examination-style question: You are applying for a job in a high street store. The store has sent you an application form. Write your answers to all sections of the form, giving the basic information required and persuading the store that you are the right person for the job.

There are many occasions when you may need to fill in an application form, for example when applying for a job or a place at college. Your audience will use your form to find out about you and to see how skilled you are at written communication.

The task form

Part 1
Name:
Address:

Date of birth:

Part 2
Schools and colleges attended:

Educational qualifications (e.g. GCSEs, Functional Skills):

Any other qualification (e.g. First Aid):

Part 3
Why you feel that you are the right person for the job:

PASS LEVEL 2 ✓

Your purpose in this form is not just to give information, although that is important. You also need to persuade the employer that you are right for the job. Your tone should still be formal, but this time it can also be persuasive and enthusiastic.

ACTIVITY

1 Copy out the form, leaving spaces for your answers.
2 Fill in Part 1 carefully, and check your work.
3 Start a page of notes. Write down your purpose and audience first.
4 Read Part 2 of the form and make notes on the information you need to include. Then fill in this part of the form and check your work.
5 Read the paragraph below, written by a student in response to Part 3.

I honestley think I'm just right for this job and you'd be a fool not to have me. I like a good laugh and chatting to people. I am carefull and sensible. I could come erly in the mornings but I'd need to have Saturday afternoons of so that I can watch my team play. My teachers say that I work hard sometimes and there right. My Mum thinks Im honest but I don't tell her everthing I do.

6 Discuss the mistakes this student has made. Think about whether:
- the content is relevant and appropriate
- the writing is accurate
- the tone is appropriate.

7 Make notes for your own response to Part 3, then write at least two paragraphs. Check your work carefully – make sure you don't make the kinds of mistakes you found in the work above.

Peer/Self-assessment

Check your finished form. What have you done well in your writing? What needs further improvement? Make corrections to your writing if you need to.

- To learn how to avoid some common spelling errors

Improve your accuracy

Common errors

The student's writing on page 81 contained some common spelling errors. Read the rules below and work through the activities to avoid making the same mistakes.

PASS LEVEL 2 ✓

Try keeping a record of the words you commonly make mistakes with. Learn how to spell them correctly. Learn and practise spelling patterns to help you to avoid making mistakes that could cost you marks in the examination.

RULE

Very few English words (apart from names for people and places) end in 'ley'. The spelling is usually 'ly'.	Incorrect I honest**ley** think	Correct I honest**ly** think
The ending 'ly' can be added to an adjective to turn it into an adverb. This means a word that tells you more about an action.	For example: To leave quick**ly**	
When full is added to another word, the second l is usually dropped.	Incorrect I am carefu**ll**	Correct I am carefu**l**
These three words sound the same but have different meanings: there their they're	**There** indicates place. For example: My application form is over th**ere** **Their** indicates possession. For example: Th**eir** forms are missing. **They're** is a short form of 'they are'. For example: Th**ey're** right.	
Off means away from.	For example: I am sending my form **off** today.	
Of means belonging to.	For example: I believe it is the fault **of** the government.	

ACTIVITY

1 Think of two adverbs ending in 'ly' to describe walking or talking.

2 Join 'full' to each word below to make correctly spelled new words:

> dread boast cheer law peace boast tear colour delight

3 Choose two of the new words and use them correctly in a sentence.

4 Choose *there*, *their* or *they're* to fill the gaps in these sentences. Choose carefully so that your sentences make sense.

> I like ____ uniform.   ____ coats are over ____.
>
> ____ going to the cinema later.
>
> ____ was nothing for ____ dinner so ____ still hungry.

5 Choose *of* or *off* to fill the gaps in this paragraph.

> I am going ____ on a training course tomorrow. It is part ____ a
>
> national scheme for making sure teachers get time ____ school.

TASK 1

It is time for you to arrange your work experience. Your school wants you to practise applying in writing to the organisation that you want to spend time in. Part of the application form is given below.

> Please explain here why you wish to do work experience in this organisation and what kind of role you would like to have. Include information on relevant qualifications and experience, and describe the personal qualities you feel will be of value to us.

Write your application.

TASK 2

You are at home when you hear a car alarm. You look out of the window and see two people breaking into your family's car. You ring the police straight away but, by the time they arrive, the two people have run away. You are asked to complete a witness statement form for the police. You should write the following information in this order.

- Your name and address.
- The time and date of the incident.
- A description of the incident, stating exactly what you heard and saw, from start to finish.
- A description of the two people.
- Any other details you think are important.

Write your form.

Study the two examples of completed forms written by students in response to the examination-style Task 2 on page 83. Use the examiner's comments to help you to assess and improve your own writing.

Student A FAIL ✗

Basic information – his surname, the date and time, his signature – is missing.

Many errors in spelling and punctuation – especially comma splices and apostrophes.

Many errors in spelling and punctuation – especially comma splices and apostrophes.

He does include some relevant details.

Many errors in spelling and punctuation – especially comma splices and apostrophes.

My name is john ✗ and yesterday ✗ while I was listning ✗ to music in my room with some mates I heard my Dads car alarm go off, ✗ I looked out the window and there was these ✗ yobs having a go at it, I got on my mobile immediately ✗ to phone you lot ✗ to come, ✗ my mates were all for going down and sorting out the yobs but I thought it might get a bit ruff ✗ so we decided to stay and watch, they were a nasty looking lot with crowbars and they smashed the cars windows and broke the areil off, ✓ I couldnt call my Dad because he was out with my mum, someone was having a go at the tires as well, it was a bit dark so i couldnt see much but I think their were two of them but they had hoods on and so there faces were difficult to see, they seemed to be average height and Id ✗ guess they were a bit older than me, ✗ thats why I wasnt keen to go and tackle them, ✗ hope this is OK. Its all I can remember.

✗

He does not stick to the required facts and includes irrelevant opinions and guesses.

The overall tone is inappropriately informal.

Basic information – his surname, the date and time, his signature – is missing.

Examiner summary

This student includes some of the required information, but the writing is vague and the points muddled. The account is not clear and the tone is too 'chatty'. The sense of audience is weak and occasionally wanders from the purpose. The report is unsigned and not dated. The answer would not gain a Level 2 pass for 'Content and organisation'.

The student makes many errors. There are comma splices throughout, and simple words are misspelt. Apostrophes are also incorrectly used. This would not gain a pass at Level 2 for 'Sentence structure, punctuation and spelling'.

Student B PASS ✓

✓ My name is Jake Brown and I live at 14 Windsor Crescent, Wakefield.

The incident occurred at 8.45 pm on 15th April 2010. ✓

I was in my bedroom when I heard a car alarm going off. I looked out of the window and saw two youths attacking my mothers ✗ car with a crowbar. ✓ I immediately called the police.

✓ They had broken the front off-side window of the car. I saw one of them lean into the car and pull out my mother's shopping bag from the front passenger seat and throw it down. They went on to attack the car aerial, ripping it out of the roof. By this time one of the youths had got the front door open and was fiddling with the ignition. He failed to start the car. ✓

✓ One of the youths was white and the other was black. Both were wearing jeans and dark T-shirts and one had a crowbar. They were of average height . ✓

I then heard the siren of a police car approaching. The youths also heard the noise and ran away down Windsor Crescent toward the main road into Wakefield.

✓ Signed Jake Brown   Date 16th April 2010

Annotations:

- Follows the format laid out in the task.
- One missing apostrophe but otherwise accurate and error-free.
- Appropriate formal tone shows strong sense of purpose and audience.
- Sticks to the facts and includes relevant details.
- Includes all the required information in the right order.
- Sticks to the facts and includes relevant details.
- Follows the format laid out in the task.

Examiner summary

This student is clear in the way he organises the information required for the form.
He follows the bullet points in the task, giving factual information without straying into unsupported opinion and irrelevant details. The tone is suitably formal and factual, and he signs and dates his report. This would gain a pass at Level 2 for 'Content and organisation'.

There is one small error, noted above, but otherwise the work is accurate in punctuation and spelling. It would gain a Level 2 pass for 'Sentence structure, punctuation and spelling'.

PASS LEVEL 2 ✓ PASS LEVEL 2

When asked to write a factual account, stick to the facts. Do not include opinions and guesses. Forms and applications will almost always be concerned only with facts.

Peer/Self-assessment

What have you have learnt about writing forms and applications? Make notes under the headings: audience, tone, format, and purpose. Is there anything you still need to improve?

Planning and persuading

TASK: To write an answer to this Functional Skills English examination-style question: Your school is involved in fundraising for a children's charity. Your year group has decided to arrange a car-boot sale. This will raise money by charging sellers for a pitch on the school playing field. You need to design a leaflet to advertise your event. Your leaflet must give information about the event, and persuade local people to support your school's chosen charity by coming to it. You should include in your leaflet:

- your choice of charity
- reasons why you think the readers should support this charity
- details about the car-boot sale, including where and when it is being held, and how readers can get more information should they wish to take part.

PASS LEVEL 2 ✔

Remember, you are writing a leaflet, not a poster. You must write enough for the examiner to assess your skills, and write in sentences.

Planning

Before you do anything else, draw up a rough plan for your answer. You can then make notes on your plan as you work through the task.

ACTIVITY 1

1 Jot down the three sections you need to write, and what you need to include.
2 Decide which charity you would like to support, and note it at the top of the page.

KEY TERMS

Your **purpose** is the reason for writing.

Your **audience** is whoever will be reading your writing.

Purpose and audience

Before you start to write, be clear on your **purpose** and **audience**. The purpose of a leaflet will usually be to inform. It will often be to persuade as well.

ACTIVITY 2

1 Read the descriptions of leaflets below. For each one, discuss its audience and purpose. Decide if each should aim just to inform, or to inform and persuade.
   - Leaflet A explains how to set up and use a new laptop.
   - Leaflet B advertises a local attraction for children.
   - Leaflet C launches a new magazine for teenagers.
2 Discuss the audience and purpose of the leaflet in the task. When you have decided what they are, note them on your plan.

PASS LEVEL 2 ✔

Always think about what your audience needs to know for you to achieve your purpose. If your writing does not meet its purpose or is inappropriate for its audience, you will not achieve Level 2.

Writing to persuade

A good persuasive leaflet will make you respond in a certain way. Its content and language will shape your views and feelings. Look again at the second bullet in the task. You need to persuade your audience that:

- your chosen charity is worth supporting
- they should come to the sale.

> **Check your tone.**
> Your writing should be clear, direct, friendly and persuasive. Make sure you are polite in the way you express ideas. Your audience will not support you if you insult them.

ACTIVITY 3

1 Suggest at least two reasons why your chosen charity is worthwhile. Think about who it helps and what good things the money raised might do. Make notes on your plan.
2 Now come up with two reasons why someone might want to attend the car-boot sale: for example, there will be plenty of great bargains on offer. Add your ideas to your notes.

Persuasive language

The text below is taken from a leaflet for Great Ormond Street Children's Hospital.

Why regular gifts make a difference

'The people here are special. They brought my son back to life. My son was dying and today he's back at school. He can play football and run round the house screaming every time Manchester United scores.' *James's Dad*

£3 a month could change children's lives
By making a regular gift of £3 a month you will make a really big difference for sick children every day. Children like 10-year-old James – his heart condition was so critical that without the expert treatment and care at Great Ormond Street Hospital, he wouldn't have survived. And there are many children like him who need our help.

Why a regular gift?
A regular gift allows us to plan for the future because we know, day in day out, that we will have a steady income stream that we can rely upon.

What do supporters receive?
As a way of keeping you up-to-date with the hospital you will receive our supporter magazine, *Lifeline*, twice a year, written by the children. *Lifeline* is packed with interviews, features and the latest news from the hospital and charity.

Annotations:

- Strong heading draws the reader in – how can the reader make a difference?
- Emotive picture and real-life example makes it harder to ignore the appeal.
- Persuasive introduction with emotive language.
- Question in the heading draws the reader in to find out the answer.
- Clear information to persuade the reader that their money will be well used.
- Persuasive offer – you get something back if you give.

ACTIVITY 4

The leaflet above is written to make people feel sympathetic and keen to help the charity. What persuasive devices are used to achieve this? Use the annotations to help you.

Writing an effective leaflet

My learning objectives ▼

- To present information clearly
- To write an effective leaflet to inform and persuade
- To check my work carefully

TASK: Remind yourself of the task on page 86 before working through this section.

Information

Your leaflet must include some essential information. You are given details of this in the third bullet point of the task. Your writing should be clear and direct – your audience wants to find the details they need quickly and easily.

PASS LEVEL 2 ✔

When writing to give information, it can help if you imagine yourself as the audience. For this task, imagine you are a local resident who might attend. What information do you need?

ACTIVITY 1

1 Re-read bullet point three of the task. Note down the required information on your plan.

Format and presentation

For this leaflet, you are directed to write in three sections in the task. To make your leaflet even clearer, you should produce a heading for each of the three sections. You may use other ways of presenting your information, such as bulleted or numbered points, subheadings, or frequently asked questions (FAQs).

ACTIVITY 2

1 Decide on your headings. They should:
   - state clearly what each section is about
   - make the reader want to read more.
2 Will it help the reader to include sub-headings? Decide on some you might put in.
3 Think about other ways of making the information easy to find.

Avoiding common mistakes

Look at this extract from a student's attempt at this task. The student makes many mistakes in the way they try to persuade the audience to support the event and give the information the audience needs to have about it.

> Dorset High School Year 10 Car boot sale
>
> It is essential that you come to our car boot sale in support of the Great Ormond Street Hospital, we feel that you should support this charitty because we don't like to think of sick children suffering. DO YOU? It would be disgusting if you didnt support us. We demand that you come to the school field on Saturday 20th July. The car boot sale starts at 2.30 and ends at 6 pm. The gates will open at 12 o'clock for cars to set up their sales pitches. There are lot's of sick children in the hospital and you will be an ungenerous person if you don't support us. You can get an application form for your car from the school office but only between 9am and 9.15 on a school day.

ACTIVITY 3

1 Discuss where this student goes wrong. Find examples of when their writing:
   - is not organised correctly and clearly into the three sections
   - is not clearly presented
   - is inappropriate in tone for its audience and purpose
   - does not give the required information
   - is inaccurate and contains errors.
2 Write a short checklist for the student of the key things to remember when writing this leaflet. The Pass Level 2 tips will give you some ideas.
3 Check your notes – have you remembered everything on your checklist? Have you made any of the same mistakes as this student? Correct your plan if you need to.

Review and write

Now use your notes to write a persuasive and informative leaflet on the fund-raising appeal.

Remember to keep your audience and purpose in mind. You will need to give the relevant information, organise and present your material clearly, and include persuasive devices.

Peer/Self-assessment

Check your finished leaflet. What have you done well in your writing? What needs further improvement? Make corrections to your leaflet if you need to.

My learning objectives ▼

- To learn about and practise using verbs
- To make sure I can use the correct verb tense
- To make sure I can match subject and verb

Improve your accuracy

Verbs

Verbs are 'doing' words. Every complete sentence must include a verb. When you are using verbs, you must be careful to make sure that you use the right tense and that your subject and verb agree. The subject is the person doing the action. The verb is what they are doing. If you have a plural subject, you need a plural verb. If you have a singular subject, you need a singular verb.

In the examination, students often make simple mistakes in grammar that lose them marks. Learn these rules for using verbs correctly. Always check your work carefully to make sure you have followed the rules.

RULES

Verb tenses

There are many different ways of talking about the past, present and future. These examples show some of the most common ways.

The present tense suggests that the action is happening now.	For example: I am sending you this leaflet for my school charity today.
The present tense can also be used to indicate a regular occurrence.	For example: I send you a leaflet for my school charity every year.
The past tense suggests that the action has already happened.	For example: I sent you a leaflet for my school charity last week.
The future tense suggests that the action has not yet happened.	For example: I will send you a leaflet for my school charity next week.

ACTIVITY

1 Read the following student's work. Look out for any errors in the subject-verb agreement and the verb tenses. Practise 'reading' in your head and check back to the rules to help you.

> Please came to our charity car boot sale in aid of Great Ormond Street Children's Hospital. The children is in desperate need of new equipment and staff to kept them healthy. It would be a tragedy if they suffered for lack of caring nurses. We has raised £1500 already and we hopes we will raise another £1000 at this sale.
>
> The event was on Saturday 10th August. The gate will open at 1pm and close at 5pm. If you wants to book a pitch or find out more, contact the school office.

If you think you might have made a mistake, 'read' the sentence in your head. Does it sound right? If it sounds wrong, check it.

2 Rewrite the paragraphs with the errors corrected. Check again to make sure that:

- you have always used the right tense for when the action takes place
- you have always used a singular verb with a singular subject OR a plural verb with a plural subject.

TASK 1

Your school is planning a talent show to raise money for sporting equipment. Write a leaflet to advertise the event.

You may want to include in your leaflet:

- the time, date and place of the show
- the different categories of competition
- entry charges
- details of the equipment wanted and how it would benefit students
- why you think people should support the show
- any other aspects you feel people should know or that might persuade them to attend.

Write your leaflet.

TASK 2

You see this notice in your local doctors' surgery.

Competition

We are offering a prize for the best leaflet aimed at encouraging people to stop smoking. All leaflets need to include the following information to persuade people to quit:

- better health
- more money to spend on other things
- better sense of taste and smell
- cleaner house and clothes
- more chance of being physically fit.

Write your leaflet.

Sometimes you will be given bullet points in your task. These bullet points are there to help you structure your answer, but they must be developed and not just copied out.

PASS LEVEL 2

Study the two examples of leaflets written by students in response to the examination-style Task 2 on page 91. Use the examiner's comments to help you to assess and improve your own writing.

Student A FAIL ✗

> Some use of layout to organise ideas but use of subheadings, picture boxes or bullet points would make the information more accessible.

✓ ✗ Smoking! is it really worth it

Clear sense of audience and purpose.

Smoking is a very addictive drug that can get you hooked after one cigarette, but is smoking really worth it? ✓

Persuasive devices are used, and the tone is appropriate.

Many people belive that smoking is non-harmful, and a 'cool' thing to do but is risking you're life really what you want to do, ✗ buying cigaretes actually costs you one fifth of your earnings, ✓ now I bet you didn't know that! So while your ✗ struggling for money that extra fifth is going to waste on cigarettes. That fifth could by you extra food, a bag you have always wanted or the trainers that are to ✗ expensive ✓

> Spelling, punctuation and sentence structures all have errors.

✓ Have you ever thought you smell of tar, ash and nicotine ✗ (or your clothes do). Well your not only killing yourself your killing your clothes and house and what people think of you. Do you want to be known as the smelly one? There is more chance of being physically fit if you don't smoke. ✓

The statistic is unrealistic.

Smoking is killing people and its ✗ getting worse. Two hundred people die from smoking every year. ✗ Are you next

> Most points from the task are included, but points are not developed, meaning the leaflet is rather short. Information about the helpline is missing.

If you want any more information ring our help line. ✓

Clear sense of audience and purpose.

✓ STOP SMOKING NOW!

Examiner summary

The student has thought about the audience by trying to persuade rather than rant at the reader. However, the leaflet is fairly short and the points made are not developed. Better use could have been made of the bullet points in the task. There is a heading at the beginning, but subheadings would have helped the writer to organise his thoughts. While it is a good idea to use statistics to support the point about the number of deaths, the choice of 200 deaths a year does not seem to be realistic. The student has a clear idea of purpose, however. Overall, this answer would not gain a Level 2 pass for 'Content and organisation'.

The first sentence is confused, and the spelling contains common errors. Punctuation is weak too, with comma splices and missing full stops and question marks. This would not gain a Level 2 pass for 'Sentence structure, punctuation and spelling'.

Student B PASS ✓

Clear layout features to make the information accessible.

✓ YOUR GUIDE TO STOPPING SMOKING

Picture of ashtray filled with cigarettes

The required points are included and developed with relevant details.

✓ Facts

Smoking is one of the main causes of illness. ✓ For example, it causes bad coughs, loss of breath, poor skin, and quicker ageing. It can cause cancer. People who start smoking at a young age and continue through life can risk heart disease and an earley ✗ death.

✓ If you give up ...

✓ * Health

Strong sense of audience and purpose.

Your health will be better. You will be able to play football without feeling ill. You will be able to live life to the full rather than being constantley ✗ getting out of breath.

Occasional errors, but mostly accurate.

* Money

Smoking costs a lot of money. Put the money you save from smoking in a jar and watch it mount up! ✓

Tone is positive and persuasive.

* Eating and drinking

Persuasive language and devices are used.

We all enjoy our food but how much of the taste of that cooked breakfast or curry are you losing because you have dulled your taste buds with smoking? Stop, wake up and taste the coffee. ✓

* Smoking smog

Every time you have a cigarette in your house you make all your furnishings and clothes smell a little worse. Do you want to be thought of as the person who always stinks of smoke?

So if you want to feel fitter, have more money in your pocket, enjoy your food and drink and smell fresh then give up smoking! Live longer and enjoy life.

Examiner summary

The student has thought carefully about the audience, using the personal appeal ('you') to involve the reader and avoiding being too critical of those who smoke. The leaflet begins with a useful section on the facts of smoking and then looks at the task bullet points, developing each point in turn. This is sensible use of the help given by the task, and also gives the leaflet a clear structure and direction. The leaflet ends with a brief summary of the points. The information is presented in a sensible and clear way, and some persuasive techniques are used. For 'Content and organisation', the candidate would gain a pass at Level 2.

The 'Sentence structure, punctuation and spelling' of the leaflet are very good. There are a few errors in spelling, but the punctuation is secure and there is a variety of sentence structures. For this aspect, the student would easily gain a Level 2 pass.

Peer/Self-assessment

What have you have learnt about writing a leaflet? Make notes under the headings: audience, tone, format and purpose. Is there anything you still need to improve?

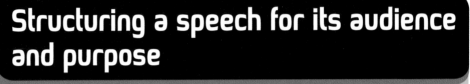

My learning objectives ▼
- To be clear about the audience and purpose of the task
- To structure and plan ideas logically

Peer/Self-assessment

Look at the learning objectives. Think about what you know and can do confidently, and what you still need to learn or practise to achieve Level 2.

Structuring a speech for its audience and purpose

TASK: To write an answer to this Functional Skills English examination-style question: The government is worried about the number of teenage drivers having crashes just after they have passed their driving test. It is proposing to raise the legal driving age to 20, by which time it believes young people are more responsible. You have been invited to write a speech for a public meeting on the subject, stating your views and persuading the meeting to agree with your view.

Purpose and audience

Always make sure that what you write meets the given purpose. Your purpose in this task is to state your opinion and persuade others to agree with it.

It is vital that you shape your arguments or information to suit your audience. This speech is for a public meeting, which means anyone can come. You therefore need to appeal to all types of people in your response. Some of the audience may think that the driving age should be raised, and others may be undecided or be against the idea. Remember, for a speech it is especially important to structure your ideas clearly – your audience cannot go back to check points they did not understand.

ACTIVITY 1

Note down the words in the task relating to audience and purpose. Check back to these as you plan your writing, to keep content and tone appropriate.

Organising and planning your ideas

There is no particular format for a speech, but your ideas and information need to be carefully organised so that the audience can follow them.

ACTIVITY 2

1 Read the extract below from a student's speech on this topic.

> Here we go again! Adults want to stop us driving. It's not us who are drink driving. At seventeen we aren't allowed in pubs anyway. Going back to my first point, it's always the same. Anything we enjoy they want to stop us. And they say we get alcohol from off licences and then pinch cars to joy ride. And then there's no public transport anyway so we can't go on it, can we? They didn't have to pass a theory test either. Another thing, we don't have lots of accidents but they do.

2 List the points the student makes, then discuss how you might organise them into a more logical order that the audience could follow more easily.

The best way to make sure your arguments are clearly organised and presented is to draft a plan before you start writing. Use it to make sure you include all your best ideas in a logical order.

You should write four or five carefully structured and easy to follow paragraphs. Your plan will help you.

ACTIVITY 3

1 Copy the plan below, leaving space to add your own notes under each heading.

> INTRODUCTION
> Paragraph 1. State briefly who you are; what you will be speaking about; what your opinion is.
>
> POINTS TO SUPPORT MY OPINION
> Paragraphs 2, 3 and 4. Developed points to support your opinion.
>
> CONCLUSION
> Paragraph 5. Restate your opinion and sum up your points to support it.

2 Write your name and the purpose of the speech under the 'Introduction' heading. Decide on your opinion: should the driving age be raised or not? Write it down next.

Make your points and back them up

You now need to think about the points you could make to support your opinion. You might include points about young people and alcohol; the driving test; public transport as an alternative to driving; how responsible young people are in other areas of their lives; and so on. Decide what arguments you could use to back up your opinions in each case.

ACTIVITY 4

1 Enter at least three of your points and arguments into your plan, under the heading 'Points to support my opinion'. You could put them in a table like the one below.

Points to support my opinion	
Point	**Argument**
1 Raising the driving age will not reduce accidents	Older people have accidents too
2	

Topic sentences

A topic sentence is one that introduces the main idea of a paragraph. Topic sentences help to structure your writing, and signal to the audience what each paragraph is about. Here are some examples of how you could start topic sentences for this speech.

> As well as this, it is also the case that ...
> I would like to tell you my views on ... and why I think you should support them.
> Finally, remember that ...
> Thirdly, I believe that ...
> My first point is ...

Make sure you use topic sentences to introduce your main ideas. This will help to make your writing clear and easy to follow.

Get the language right

- To learn to use an appropriate tone
- To write persuasively

KEY TERM

Tone is the style of writing and language you use.

Successful speeches use effective persuasive language

The right tone

If you want to persuade people, then you need to get them on your side. You will not do this if they are upset by the **tone** you use. Nobody is impressed with language that is rude or abrupt.

Writing can be funny, serious, informal, formal or angry, for example. These are all tones. Think carefully about the tone of your writing. Check your audience and purpose to help you decide what kind of tone is required for the task.

ACTIVITY 1

1 Look at these pairs of extracts from speeches. In both pairs, the same point is made but in a different tone. Decide which sentence in each pair uses an appropriate tone and which would not impress an audience.

> I think all those oldies who say we shouldn't drive are off their heads.
> *The views of the older generation should be taken into account, but …*
>
> Not all young people are irresponsible drivers of high-powered cars.
> *Only an imbecile would let a kid drive a car.*
>
> In my experience, it is not only teenagers who like to drink alcohol.
> *Us teens are not as drunk and stupid as some older folk.*

2 How could you rewrite the following sentences in a more appropriate tone?

> At least teenagers have got enough brain power left to pass a driving test.
> The buses are rubbish, they're always late and packed out.
> If you disagree with me, it's obvious you haven't listened to a word I've said.

Persuasive language

There are a number of persuasive devices that you can use which will help you to win over your audience.

- **Rhetorical question** – a question to which you supply the answer, or to which the answer is obvious. It can help to persuade when listeners agree with the answer and therefore feel they are 'on your side'.
- **Repetition** – using the same words or sentence structure several times for effect.
- **Emotive language** – powerful words that appeal to the audience's emotions.
- **Statistics** – backing up your points with facts and figures.
- **Anecdotes** – backing up your points with examples from your own or others' lives.

ACTIVITY 2

1 Read the extract below from a speech on this subject. Spot examples of the persuasive devices used.

> We can get married at the age of 16. We can be a teenage parent. We can join the army at 17. Why can't we drive? It seems to me that if we are considered old enough to take on major responsibilities like marriage, parenting and dying for our country, then we are old enough to drive.
>
> Young people are often called irresponsible drivers. On the other hand, I often see older men reeling out of the pub and getting into their over-powered cars to drive home. Is this responsible? Statistics suggest that a drunken driver is more likely to be in his thirties or forties than his teens. These older drivers are much more likely to kill your son or daughter, your mother or father, than a teenage driver.

2 Copy and complete the table with details of the persuasive devices you have spotted.

Device	Examples
Rhetorical question	
Repetition	
Emotive language	
Statistics	
Anecdotes	

3 Now go back to the notes you have made under the heading 'Points to support my opinion'. For each one, think of how you could use persuasive devices to support your point. Look back at the examples in your table to help you.

For each point you make, ask yourself:
- Am I stating my opinion clearly?
- Am I giving good reasons for others to agree with my opinion?
- Am I using polite and persuasive language?

Review and write

Now put together all you have learnt and practised, and write your speech. Remember to:

- write with your purpose and audience in mind, using your plan to structure your speech
- use your notes to make at least three points, backing them up with good arguments
- introduce each new point with a topic sentence
- write politely and persuasively
- write a conclusion, restating your opinion and summing up your arguments.

Peer/Self-assessment

Check your finished speech. What have you done well in your writing? What needs further improvement? Make corrections to your speech if you need to.

Improve your accuracy

Peer/Self-assessment

Look back at your finished speech. Are your sentences accurate and varied? Make corrections if you need to.

In the examination, you will need to show that you can use correctly a range of different sentence structures, including complex sentences. This will make your work more interesting and gain you marks.

Different kinds of sentences

You need to be able to use a range of different types of sentence to make your writing interesting. Aim to use a mixture of simple, compound and complex sentences.

RULES

Type of sentence	Subject verb
Simple sentence A simple sentence is a sentence that contains a subject and a verb. Simple sentences can be clear and effective, but if you use them all the time your work will become boring.	Young people should drive at 17. Cameras have been installed at the school.
Compound sentence A compound sentence is made up of simple sentences joined with: *and, but or or.*	Young people should drive at 17 but they should not carry passengers. Cameras have been installed in school and I agree with this decision.
Complex sentence A complex sentence is made up of simple sentences joined with words such as: *although, as, because, if, since, though, until, when, where, whereas.* [NOT *however, nevertheless* as this leads to comma splicing.]	Young people should drive at 17, although they should be tested on their driving skills first. Young people should drive at 17 if we want a fair system. Cameras have been installed in school because vandalism was increasing .

Full stops

ACTIVITY

Correct this student's work. Replace all the comma splices with full stops or by creating different kinds of sentences.

We should be allowed to drive at the age of 17, if you live in a village the buses only come several times a day, you can't get to college on time. It's not right that we have to rely on our parents for lifts all the time, they have their lives to lead as well. They don't want to be carting us about all the time, we should be allowed to take our test and be independent.

TASK 1

Your school has installed a number of surveillance cameras, both within and outside the building, to reduce vandalism and improve behaviour. This means your movements can be tracked around school. It has also set up airport-style metal detectors at the main entrances.

The Governors of the school have called an open meeting to discuss people's opinions on these measures. You have been chosen to make a speech to the governors. You should inform them of the views of your year group, and persuade them to bring their policies in line with those views.

You may like to include the following points in your speech:

- whether the cameras have stopped the vandalism
- whether the metal detectors make the students and staff feel safer in school
- the effect on personal freedom when people's movements are recorded
- the cost of installing and maintaining the equipment
- other resources the money could have been spent on
- anything else you think is important.

Write your speech.

TASK 2

Your local council is holding an open meeting to discuss facilities for young people in your area. You have been invited to give a speech on behalf of people your age, informing the meeting of the facilities currently available and persuading the council as to how and why they should be improved.

You may like to include:

- details of existing facilities
- facilities you would like to be added
- the benefits of improving the facilities
- any other points you feel are relevant.

Write your speech.

Study the two examples of speeches written by students in response to the examination-style Task 2 on page 99. Use the examiner's comments to help you to assess and improve your own writing.

Student A FAIL ✗

The tone is inappropriately informal.

Many errors, and sentences are long and muddled.

Language is too informal for the audience.

Points are muddled and sometimes irrelevant.

I want to talk to you tonite ✗ about the facilities for young kids in our area, ✗ I don't think there are enough because lots of young people have to hang around on street corners and ✓ this isn't good because they start to drink and get into trouble. We should have a lot more youth clubs which are open every day of the week and it would be good to have a skateboard park some where near where I live ✗ because I like doing that and so do my mates, ✗ the football pitches in the parks are rubbish to. ✗ They are just mud baths and the posts are always broken from kids swinging on them, when we go in the park we always get told of ✗ by the park keeper for being a nuisance, all we want is a game of footie. ✗ We arent welcome in the shopping precint either because there is always police hanging around watching what we do. Theres ✗ nowhere for us to go and enjoy ourselves and ✗ we are fed up with it. Why carnt ✗ we have some where to go?

Points are sometimes backed up but often only by opinions not facts.

Many errors, and sentences are long and muddled.

Language is too informal for the audience.

Examiner summary

The student's understanding of audience is weak. The speech begins inappropriately and the points are muddled, sometimes straying from the task and introducing irrelevant details. Little notice is taken of the bullet points in the task, which would have given the writer a clear structure for the speech. The tone is too informal, and opportunities to develop the points made or to persuade the council using well-developed views are missed. This answer would not gain a Level 2 pass for 'Content and organisation'.

There are a number of mistakes, both in spelling and punctuation. Comma splicing and uncertainty in apostrophe usage reduce the marks, as does misspelling of simple words. The writing would not gain a Level 2 pass for 'Sentence structure, punctuation and spelling'.

Student B PASS ✓

Good evening, ladies and gentlemen. ✓ My name is Anya and I want to give you a young person's view of the recreational facilities in this area. ✓

✓ First, I would like to look at the facilities that already exist. There is a good swimming pool on the High Street but the opening times are limited and often it is booked out to clubs such as mothers and toddlers groups. This means that in holiday times we're not free to go when we like. I appreciate that it sometimes needs to be closed to the general public, but it would be good if it could be open later in the evening instead. The Leisure Centre is excellent, but again different clubs have often block-booked facilities. I think it is important that the fitness suites should be open to the public at all times. Lots of young people want to keep fit but don't want to play team games, and the Fitness Suite is ideal for this. ✓

The parks are excellent for a walk, but the upkeep of the pitches is poor and I know this discourages young people from using these areas. There are some youth clubs, but the opening hours are restricted to two or three nights a week. If you want to keep young people off the streets, it may be a good idea to have them open more frequently. ✓ If there is nowhere else to go, it isn't surprising that young people gather on street corners, and this sometimes leads to trouble.

Secondly, I should like to see certain improvements. As I have suggested, some facilities need to be open longer or more frequently. Added to this, I believe that the youth in the area would be more contented and less likely to make trouble if they had more facilities to enjoy and use. I know many young people would like a skateboard park where they could practise their skills. This could be set up in the town park without great expense. Others would like the park to be properly maintained so that they can have a game of soccer on a decent pitch. Many young people need advice on things that they don't want to discuss with their parents and I think that the town should open a drop-in centre where they could get advice from trained advisers. ✓ ✗

✓ To sum up, I believe that the situation would be better if just a little money were spent on improving the present facilities. I think a number of them should be open for longer and that new ones need to be added. I believe that this would reduce vandalism and ill-behaviour in our town. ✓ Thank you for listening to me.

> Clear sense of audience and purpose.

> Clear organisation through introduction, numbered points and conclusion.

> Points made are well backed up with detail and are made persuasively.

> Suggestions are made, but this section is a little rushed – the student may have not have allowed enough time to complete this part of the work.

> Points made are well backed up with detail and are made persuasively.

Examiner summary

This is competent work. The student has understood the need for clear organisation, and the sentence starters ('First', 'Secondly', 'To sum up') help this. In places the speech is repetitive, but there is a good understanding of the audience and the tone is calm and thoughtful. The bullet points in the task are all covered, although a few more suggestions could have been included, and the benefits of improving the facilities aspect is a little rushed. The student does, however, try to persuade the council to make changes and gives the benefits of doing so. This would gain a Level 2 pass for 'Content and organisation'.

The student can write clearly and accurately, and uses a range of sentence structures. This piece would gain a pass at Level 2 for 'Sentence structure, punctuation and spelling'.

Assessment

Introduction

Your Functional Skills English assessments are designed to test your ability to communicate every day to get the most out of life, learning and work.

Your skills are assessed across:

Reading
Writing
Speaking, listening and communication

You must achieve Level 2 in all three areas to be awarded a Level 2 Pass.

Why do you need to pass Level 2?

- To equip you with practical 'real-life' communication skills that employers need.
- Because the skills you use for Functional English form a significant part of what you need to succeed in GCSE English and English Language.
- Because the skills you learn can be used in other subjects.
- Because Functional English aims to promote learner independence.
- Because a Level 2 pass is half a GCSE at C grade.

How will you be assessed?

You will take examinations for Reading and Writing, and be assessed by your teacher for Speaking, listening and communication. Details of the different assessments are given later in this section, but remember:

- You can retake each component if you need to – so, for example, if you reach Level 2 in Reading and Writing but not Speaking, listening and communication, you only have to retake Speaking, listening and communication.
- You do not need to produce any coursework.
- Reading, Writing, and Speaking, listening and communication are of equal assessment value and you need to pass all three.

How will you be assessed for Reading?

Reading is assessed in a one-hour examination.

- In the examination, you will be given three texts to read and use to answer questions. These texts are usually linked by a topic or theme, though the writers may have different points of view.
- The texts will always be non-fiction, and might include articles, instructions, web pages, reports, leaflets, letters, and so on. They might be on topics that you are familiar with, such as health or the environment – but remember you are only being tested on your reading skills, not on your knowledge of the topic.
- The questions will be in a booklet. All questions require a written response, and there will be spaces in the booklet for you to write your answers.
- All questions will have a mark next to them. This should help you work out how much to write in your answer. For example, if a question asking you to 'list' is worth ten marks, you should include ten different points in your answer.
- Sometimes the answer boxes will have bullet points or a table for you to complete. Make sure you use the required format in your answer.
- The number and type of questions, and the marks allocated to them, will vary from paper to paper.

Understanding the questions

Search for key words in the questions to work out exactly what you are being asked to do and what reading skills you need to use. For example:

| A clear direction to use your summarising skills. | Summarise the common symptoms experienced by people suffering from depression, according to the web page. [10] | A clear direction on what to summarise – the common symptoms. Leave out everything else. |

| Make sure you use the right text – here, you are directed to use the web page given. | | There are ten marks – you need to make ten points. |

Five strategies for Reading success

1	Read the questions carefully and find the key words – then use them in your answer, so the examiner knows you are focused on answering exactly what has been asked.
2	When looking for information, follow the text in the order in which it is written – if you jump around the page, you could end up missing out important points. Use skimming, scanning and close reading skills to find the points you need.
3	Many students repeat themselves in their answers – this will not earn you any extra marks. Make sure you plan and check your answers and cross out any points that are repeated.
4	Make sure you write enough. Check how many marks each question is worth and include that many points from the texts. Don't include any points from your own knowledge – you will not get any marks for them.
5	Read the questions carefully to check which text or texts you need to use in each answer. If you use the wrong ones, you will get no marks, however good your answer is.

Home | About Us | Sitemap | Contact Us

Search this site... [GO]

88 Visitors Online

TeenIssues

- Ask Our Experts
- Diet & Fitness
- Environmental Issues
- Family Life
- Friends & Relationships
- Get A Life
- Mental Health
- Physical Health
- School Life
- Self Harming
- Teenage Troubles
- Site Information
- Readers Comments

Our Newsletter

To receive our free monthly newsletter please enter your email address below:

[OK]

Get the latest TeenIssues updates

RSS Feed
Add to Google
MY YAHOO!

Teenage Depression

Have you been feeling tired, lazy, lonely and sad? Does staying in bed all day seem preferable to going out into the world? Do the things that once made you smile now just seem to annoy you? If you answered yes to any of these questions, and these symptoms have been occurring consistently for a few weeks, then you might be depressed. Depression is no laughing matter (pardon the bad pun), so make sure you get the help you deserve by visiting your GP immediately.

What is Depression?

There are many common symptoms of depression, though people suffering from depression may not exhibit them all. These symptoms include:

- unsettled or lack of sleep
- an overwhelming feeling of tiredness
- an increase in 'sleeping in' or afternoon naps
- difficulty concentrating throughout the day
- loss of interest in favourite or previously entertaining activities
- avoidance of classes, clubs, sports teams or social events
- decrease in school work and performance
- feeling unable to become motivated or enthusiastic about anything
- loss of, or excessive increase in, appetite
- rapid weight loss or gain
- inability to picture the future
- general loss of hope, or feeling like giving up
- little effort put into personal hygiene or appearance
- believing that life isn't worth living or having suicidal thoughts.

How is Clinical Depression Diagnosed?

Visiting your GP is the first step towards diagnosing and alleviating depression. During your appointment you will need to be honest with your GP about your behaviour and emotions, and (s)he will most likely ask you questions about how you are feeling, your life and any major events that have occurred recently. Your GP may suggest a course of counselling or therapy and refer you to a psychologist or other specialist.

How is Depression Treated?

The good news about depression is that there are many options for treatment and all of them have good results. Depending on your circumstances, your doctor may recommend:

- counselling to treat any underlying issues
- cognitive behaviour therapy, or 'talk therapy' that can help you change the way you think and react to situations
- more exercise and a better diet to give you a firm foundation for health
- holistic therapies such as massage or aromatherapy for a natural boost
- medication to treat your symptoms.

TEEN ADVICE, ISSUES & HELP PAGES

| HOME | ABOUT | ASK | PRIVACY POLICY | | 🔍 |

17
DEC/09

James' Story

Before year 10, I'd always spent my free time playing sport. Now, I was expected to study every night. My older sister had done well at school so my parents expected the same from me, and mum was always checking on me. I missed training sessions due to coursework deadlines so I was dropped as rugby captain. My mates teased me about this which made me really unhappy. The worst thing was when my girlfriend dumped me. She said I was 'no fun' and 'boring'. Everything was falling apart ... It didn't occur to me that I was depressed. Stuff like that's for losers, right?

Looking back, my first symptom of depression was feeling tired constantly. I couldn't concentrate and I wasn't bothered with mates. I missed deadlines at school and pretended I didn't care – inside I was gutted. Stopping eating and avoiding school finally got me noticed.

Mum's friend is my art teacher. One day, he mentioned my symptoms and told me that he had suffered from depression after a car accident. It was a relief to know that he had felt the same.

I saw the doctor and she diagnosed depression. I was embarrassed and made her promise not to tell anyone. The doctor sent me for counselling. It really helped and now I can talk about my experiences to friends. I still have 'down days' but now I know how to handle my feelings. I'm more relaxed about school and stick to a timetable to get everything done.

I now realise that depression is not for losers – it can happen to anyone. My advice is to get professional help and feel reassured that you are not alone.

Tired all the time?

Can't concentrate?

Life no fun any more?

You may be suffering from depression.

Depression can affect anyone, at any time. Don't suffer alone – talk to your GP. Your doctor can help you, by being someone to share your feelings with in confidence, arranging counselling or, if things get really bad, prescribing something to help.

If you think you may be depressed, make an appointment with your doctor, now.

Paper 1

(40 marks)

In this paper you will be assessed for your reading and understanding skills. You will need to use the resource materials: 'Teenage Depression' web page, 'James' Story' blog and 'Tired all the time?' poster.

1 Summarise the common symptoms experienced by people suffering from depression, according to the web page 'Teenage Depression'. [10]

2 The web page 'Teenage Depression' aims to help teenagers who are suffering from depression. How does it try to do this? [10]

3 According to the web page, 'Teenage Depression', and the poster, 'Tired all the time?', how might your GP treat depression? [5]

4 What caused James' depression, according to the article 'James' Story'? [5]

5 What do you think is the purpose of the article 'James' Story'? Give reasons for your answer. [4]

6 Now that you have read all the resource materials, write some advice for a friend who you think is suffering from depression. [6]

Examiner tips

Read the questions

Read each question carefully. Then read it again, and highlight the key words.

ACTIVITY 1

The examiner has already highlighted question 1 for you. Look at the words they have highlighted and read their notes carefully.

Write a summary.

Only include common symptoms – nothing else.

1. Summarise the common symptoms experienced by people suffering from depression, according to the web page 'Teenage Depression'. [10]

Just use this text, not 'James' Story' or your own knowledge.

There are ten marks available. Make sure you make ten clear points.

Always highlight the key words in a question. Then use the key words in your answers to show that you are focused on what the examiner wants.

Reading skills

Remember to use all your reading skills:

- Skim to find the main idea of the text.
- Skim to search for particular information that is asked for.
- Scan to search for particular information or key words.
- Close read to find information in detail.
- Highlight the relevant parts of the text that you need to answer each question.
- Use your highlights to summarise points effectively and without missing anything.
- Make sure you are clear about the purpose of the text and why the audience might be reading it.

ACTIVITY 2

Practise answering the questions in the paper opposite. Use the tips on this page to help you.

Look for clues on exactly how to respond in the questions and in the answer booklet. For example, you might be asked for a summary, list, table or paragraph.

Study the answers below to the examination-style Reading tasks on page 106. Use the examiner's comments to work out what you need to do to pass, and to help you assess and improve your own reading skills.

Student A FAIL ✗

1   Summarise the common symptoms experienced by people suffering from depression, according to the web page 'Teenage Depression'. [10]

> Unsettled or lack of sleep. ✗
> An overwhelming feeling of tiredness.
> An increase in 'sleeping in' or afternoon naps.
> Difficulty concentrating throughout the day.
> Loss of interest in favourite or previously entertaining activities.
> Avoidance of classes, clubs, sports teams or social events. ✗

Question asks for a summary, not a list.

Not enough points made to gain ten marks.

Examiner summary

This candidate has not picked up on the key word in the question – 'Summarise' – and has wrongly written a list instead. They have not checked the marks available for the question – for ten marks they need to make ten points, but they have only made six.

2   The web page 'Teenage Depression' aims to help teenagers who are suffering from depression. How does it try to do this? [10]

> ✗ It gives us a web address at the bottom of the page to help us if we need more information. ✓ The website includes a list of symptoms to help teenagers know if they have depression. There is also a picture of a normal girl ✓ to help show us that anyone can be depressed. It also tells teenagers what depression is so we know what it is. The website uses headings ✓ to help teenagers find the information they need easily.

Wrong order – this point comes last on the page.

Some valid points.

Mention of layout features and illustration.

Examiner summary

This candidate has some good ideas. They link the answer to the question and show not just what is in the article but also how it achieves its purpose. However, the order of the information is not helpful as the candidate jumps around the page and this is possibly why they have missed a number of points. The answer also needs to cover more information to achieve a Level 2 – checking the marks allocated would have helped the student to include the right number of points.

3 According to the web page 'Teenage Depression', and the poster 'Tired all the time?' how might your GP treat depression? [5]

Counselling ✗

Exercise

Medication

> Only three points made.

Examiner summary

This candidate does not seem to have noticed the number of marks on offer – there are only three items in the answer, when there are five possible marks. In addition, the question did not ask for a list – shortening the answers in this way does not give a clear idea of what the treatments are. The candidate has not demonstrated that they have used both texts as directed.

4 What caused James' depression, according to the article 'James' Story'? [5]

James' depression is caused because ✓ his mates were winding him up about his rugby. He also felt down because he had so much work to do. The final thing was when he got dumped by his girlfriend. ✗

> Using own words.

> Answer is too short.

Examiner summary

This candidate clearly understands some of the reasons behind James' depression, but they need to include more detail. The explanations could be clearer, but the candidate is sensible to put the reasons into their own words.

5 What do you think is the purpose of the article 'James' Story'? Give reasons for your answer. [4]

✗ James is really depressed and needs help with his counselling. I think that by writing his story it will help him because he will feel that he is sharing his ideas with other people and it might get him his girlfriend back if she understands what he went through. ✗

> Does not address the question.

> Points made that are not in the text.

Examiner summary

The first sentence shows the examiner that this candidate has not read and understood the question or picked up on the key word 'purpose' in it. The answer includes information that is not in the text, which will gain no marks.

6 Now that you have read all the resource materials, write some advice for a friend who you think is suffering from depression. [6]

✓ If you are depressed the advice I would give you is to get out more and to try and forget all of your worries. It would be a good idea to see the doctor to get some pills if you need them. I also think you should relax and take it easy and not get stressed. I think you need to stop drinking ✗ as you might become even more down once you are drunk.

> Answer is focused on the question.

> This point is not made in the text.

Examiner summary

Although there are some sensible points here, a number of the ideas are not linked to the article or web page – it is sensible not to drink, but this is based on the candidate's knowledge and not from their reading of the texts. The language could draw more from the text. For example, it would be better to write 'medication' rather than 'pills'. A close fail – the candidate just needs to be more specific.

PASS LEVEL 2

Study the answers below to the examination-style Reading tasks on page 106. Use the examiner's comments to work out what you need to do to pass, and to help you assess and improve your own reading skills.

Student B PASS ✓

1 Summarise the common symptoms experienced by people suffering from depression, according to the web page 'Teenage Depression'. [10]

> ✓ Common symptoms of depression are that you will feel unsettled; you will also feel tired and feel like you lack sleep. Many people will nap and will find it difficult to concentrate. Some people will lose interest in their hobbies and will even avoid school. Some people give up hope and might even feel suicidal if suffering from depression.

Clear reference to the question.

Examiner summary

This candidate has read the question carefully and written a focused summary. They have included many of the symptoms and have managed to condense them into a short but very clear summary. The symptoms are well connected using 'and', which allows the candidate to score more than one mark in each sentence.

2 The web page 'Teenage Depression' aims to help teenagers who are suffering from depression. How does it try to do this? [10]

> ✓ The website aims to make teenagers aware of depression and aims to give us information about its causes and what we can do if we are suffering. ✓ The picture at the top of the page is of a normal girl and this ✓ helps teenagers who are suffering as they realise that anyone can be depressed. The layout is also useful as the text has clear headings ✓ 'What is Depression?' and this helps us find the right section quickly and easily. Bullet points of symptoms are helpful and easy to follow, e.g. 'lack of sleep'. The web page is also ✓ helpful as following the symptoms it tells teenagers how depression is treated so they can immediately see what can be done and how they can be helped. The article does use some medical language 'Cognitive behaviour therapy' but it is helpful ✓ as it then explains what this means. The article gives a web address at the bottom of the page and this is helpful as we know where to find more information.

Clear link to the question.

Good reference to how layout and picture contribute to purpose.

Good use of quotes.

Repeated use of key word 'help' from the question.

Examiner summary

This candidate includes many of the same points as the previous candidate, but their answer is systematic, well focused and clearly linked to the question. They select an area of the text which they feel is helpful and then explain why it will be of use to teenagers. The constant use of the words 'helps' and 'helpful' is a clear sign that this candidate is constantly focused on the question.

3 According to the web page 'Teenage Depression', and the poster 'Tired all the time?' how might your GP treat depression? [5]

> Your GP might treat depression using the following: ✓
> * Counselling – to discover any causes ✓
> * Cognitive behaviour therapy – where you talk through your problems
> * Suggesting you do more exercise and make sure you are eating properly
> * Giving you someone to talk to in confidence
> * Medication

> Answers expanded with relevant details.

> Clear link to key words from the question.

Examiner summary This candidate includes a clear and focused introduction to show what they are writing about. They have also realised that the question is about 'locating information' so have used bullet points to help the reader. They have put the treatments into their own words, but include enough detail to ensure the examiner knows that they understand. They have used both texts as directed.

4 What caused James' depression, according to the article 'James' Story'? [5]

> James' depression ✓ was caused by a number of things at home and in school.
> These include:
> * Expectations of year 10
> * Pressure from parents and teachers
> * Pressure of being compared to an older sister
> * Dropped as rugby captain
> * Losing his girlfriend ✓

> Key word from the question.

> Full and clear list – five points made for five marks.

Examiner summary A very comprehensive list of reasons, clearly linked to the question.

5 What do you think is the purpose of the article 'James' Story'? Give reasons for your answer. [4]

> I think that the purpose ✓ of James' story is to share his experience with other people; I think this ✓ because at the end he says 'feel reassured that you are not on your own'. I also think the purpose of his story is to show that this is common and can happen to anyone as he repeats the word 'losers' to show that he has now changed his opinion. Another purpose of James' story might be to inform others about depression and the things that can cause it but also how it can be treated, e.g. 'The doctor sent me for counselling.'

> Key word.

> Points are backed up with evidence from the text.

Examiner summary The first sentence shows that the candidate is focused on the question. They give a number of alternative purposes for the text, and these are backed up with sensible examples and reasons.

6 Now that you have read all the resource materials, write some advice for a friend who you think is suffering from depression. [6]

> After talking to you, I think you may be suffering from depression. I have done some research and have some advice ✓ for you. I think you should see a doctor or talk to a counsellor to understand why you are depressed. I would also advise you to take any medication prescribed by the doctor. You really shouldn't be embarrassed – you need to talk about your feelings. It might help to do some exercise or your usual activities to help you get back to normal. ✓

> Clear link to question.

> Points made are all from the texts.

Examiner summary A comprehensive selection of advice based on information from all the articles.

How will you be assessed for Speaking, listening and communication?

- There is no examination for Speaking, listening and communication. Tasks will be set and assessed in your school or place of learning.
- The tasks will be chosen by your teachers and will be based on 'real-life' situations.
- You may be asked to work individually, in pairs or in groups.
- To achieve a pass at Level 2, you must take part in a discussion and give a presentation.
- You will need to take on a range of roles. This does not mean acting a part. It simply means contributing in different ways, e.g. as a discussion leader, speaker, listener, and so on.
- You may be working with an unfamiliar person or context in your discussion, e.g. an interviewer from outside of your school. Just remember the skills you have learned and apply them whatever the situation.

Understanding the tasks

Search for key words in the tasks to work out exactly why you are speaking, who you are speaking to, and what you need to include.

This is a clear direction that you need to prepare a presentation – other tasks may ask you to take a particular role in a discussion.

Prepare a presentation for Year 5 pupils at a local primary school to inform them about global warming.

This is a clear direction on who your audience is. Make sure you adapt your language and the information you include to suit the audience.

Your topic is global warming – make sure you stick to it and don't include irrelevant information.

In this case your purpose is to inform – not to persuade. Use appropriate language.

Ten strategies for Speaking, listening and communication success

1	Before you start planning out your response, analyse the task carefully. There could be more than one possible response.
2	You must work out the purpose and audience of the task, and your own objectives. This will help you present the right information to the right people in the right way, and use the correct level of formality for your purpose and audience.
3	The topic or situation for the tasks may be new or unfamiliar. Make sure you know exactly what you need to include before you begin. You are expected to give a range of different ideas, and to develop the level of detail you include to achieve a pass at Level 2.
4	Don't try to write down every word you intend to say. You should not read your answer out. Instead, use bullet points and the key words/phrases that you want to include.
5	Don't include anything that is not on your plan unless it is directly relevant. This will help you to stick to your point and come across as clear and organised.
6	Don't give one-word answers. Make sure you have enough to say without repeating yourself.
7	Show that you understand the whole topic and different points of view.
8	Make sure you speak politely, that you can be heard, that you listen carefully to the points made by other people, and that you involve others by asking questions.
9	Always use your speaking, listening and communication skills to move the discussion forward.
10	Make sure you know a range of persuasive techniques to help you persuade others, if appropriate.

PRACTICE TASK 1

You have applied for a job waiting on tables in a local restaurant. Prepare a presentation to tell the interviewers about yourself, and why you believe you have the necessary skills for the job.

ACTIVITY 1

1 Analyse the task for the key words. Jot down:
   - the purpose
   - the audience
   - the situation.
2 What sort of language would you use?
3 What kind of information do you think you would prepare? List five points.

Student A

Student A has prepared a plan for their presentation in response to this task.
Read their notes and the examiner's comments.

Student has read the task correctly.

More details needed on what the student can offer.

Notes for presentation
- A summary of me
- What has prepared me for the job?
- Respond to the skills needed
  - Greeting customers and allocating tables
  - Taking customer orders and informing the chef of meal choices
  - Serving food
  - Organising bills and taking payment
Other supporting Information

Includes the points asked for in the right order. Bullets make it easy to follow.

More prompts could be useful so nothing is forgotten.

List needed so that nothing is missed.

Examiner summary

The areas the student aims to cover seem sensible and clear. It would be useful to add a few key words to support each of the bullet points, as most of this plan simply retells the application information. They might want to list the supporting information, or use key words to prompt what they want to say. This is always sensible because it is easy to forget important points in pressurised situations.

For this task, the student would need to remember to be polite and speak formally.
They should use language that both informs the interviewers about themselves, and also persuades the interviewers that they are the right person for the job.

ACTIVITY 2

1 Use the examiner's comments to think about what you might change on your own plan.
2 Practise using your plan to give your presentation.

PRACTICE TASK 2

Last weekend you witnessed an accident on the road. The police want to interview you to find out exactly what you saw. Plan a presentation for them about this incident.

ACTIVITY 1

1 Analyse the task for the key words. Jot down:
   - the purpose
   - the audience
   - the situation.
2 What sort of language would you use?
3 What kind of information do you think you would prepare? List five points.

Student B

Student B has prepared a mind map for their presentation in response to this task. They have included a word bank of key terms they might use. Read their notes and the examiner's comments.

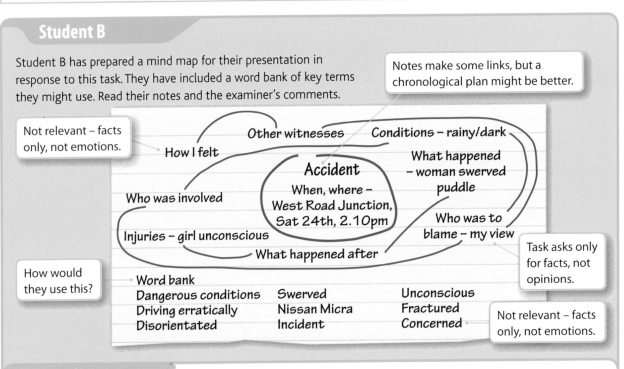

Notes make some links, but a chronological plan might be better.

Not relevant – facts only, not emotions.

How I felt

Other witnesses   Conditions – rainy/dark

What happened – woman swerved puddle

Accident
When, where – West Road Junction, Sat 24th, 2.10pm

Who was involved

Who was to blame – my view

Injuries – girl unconscious

What happened after

Task asks only for facts, not opinions.

How would they use this?

Word bank
Dangerous conditions   Swerved   Unconscious
Driving erratically   Nissan Micra   Fractured
Disorientated   Incident   Concerned

Not relevant – facts only, not emotions.

Examiner summary

The candidate has clearly thought through what information would be needed. Using two different prompts could create a lack of fluency as they move between different notes. The information does not seem to follow any order. This would not be useful in a formal presentation in which clear details are needed. A flow chart might be better. It would give the information in order, and extra details could be added to support the central ideas.

For this task, the student must avoid emotion – the purpose is simply to give clear, accurate information in formal language.

ACTIVITY 2

1 Use the examiner's comments to think about what you might change on your own plan.
2 Practise using your plan to give your presentation.

PRACTICE TASK 3

There have been a number of complaints about disruptive behaviour by teenagers in your local community. The police and council want to trial a curfew for all under 16s for three months. This would mean teenagers up to the age of 16 would have to stay at home between 9 pm and 7 am, unless they are with an adult.

There is to be public meeting to discuss the curfew proposal, and you have volunteered to join it. Prepare for and have the discussion.

ACTIVITY 1

1 Analyse the task for the key words. Jot down:
   - the purpose
   - the audience
   - the situation.
2 What sort of language would you use?

Points of view

Most young people will oppose the curfew and have similar ideas about why they do not like the idea. You could take this position, or you might like to try a different viewpoint to make your contributions more interesting. Here are two suggestions:

- You might agree with the curfew because you are concerned about teenage crime.
- You might make the point that responsible teenagers will not be able to have part-time jobs in the evenings if there is a curfew.

ACTIVITY 2

Decide on the viewpoint you will take. Make notes of key points you want to make.

Running the discussion

Remember, you need to:
- decide on a chairperson
- take on a range of roles: speaking, listening, questioning, supporting, summarising
- use appropriate language to make your points clearly
- listen carefully to all viewpoints. You can change your own if you are convinced by someone else's points.

ACTIVITY 3

Practise using your notes to have the discussion.

How will you be assessed for Writing?

- Writing is assessed in a one-hour examination.
- In the examination, you will be given two writing tasks. These tasks are not usually linked by a topic or theme, and are not linked to the reading section of the exam.
- You will always be asked to write non-fiction texts based on real-life situations, such as reports, formal or informal letters, emails, forms or applications, leaflets, speeches, and so on.
- Each task will be worth 20 marks. You are awarded marks for the following:
  - Content and organisation (11 marks).
  - Sentence structure, spelling, and punctuation (9 marks).
- You will usually be expected to write around 300 – 350 words per task.

Understanding the questions

Spend a couple of minutes reading each question and thinking about how you will respond. You must consider the following ideas as a starting point:

- Purpose – why am I writing and what do I need to include to achieve my aims? Do I only need to inform, or to persuade as well?
- Audience – who am I writing for?
- Format – how will I structure my answer (what will it look like)?
- Tone – does my writing need to be formal or informal?

This is an example of a Writing task, with annotations made by a student.

Format – I will need to follow the format of the form.

You have decided to apply for a place in a new reality TV show. You need to complete the part of the application <u>form</u> in which you <u>persuade</u> the <u>producers</u> that you would be <u>entertaining</u> if you were to join the show.

My audience is the producers.

Tone – it is a formal application but I also want to show I am entertaining.

My purpose is to persuade them to give me a place.

Now look at these notes the examiner has made for you. Read them carefully, then attempt the task.

Purpose – to complete an application form and paragraph to persuade the producers that you are suitable for their show.

Audience – the audience is the producers of the show – think about the kind of person they would be looking for.

Format – the application form will have sections for you to complete, so you must complete them all. For the 100 words there is no suggested format. It would be sensible to write down your ideas in a clear paragraph.

Tone – this is a tricky one. You don't know the producers and you want them to take your application seriously, but a formal tone would be too serious for entertaining writing. Use quite a lively tone, but avoid slang and other informal conventions.

Ten strategies for Writing success

1	Read the questions carefully and find the key words that tell you about your purpose, audience, format and tone. The question will usually tell you what format to use – make sure you write exactly what you are asked for. Keep referring back to your audience, purpose, format and tone to make sure you stay on task.
2	Write a brief plan so that your writing is logically structured. Remember, your plan is to help you to stay organised – you will not get any marks for it so keep it short. Include all the points you have been given in the question, and your own ideas as well.
3	Make sure you adapt your style of writing to your purpose and audience – remember, you would not use the same language to chat to children as to make a presentation to your headteacher.
4	Aim to write four or five complete paragraphs. Jot down on your plan what each paragraph will cover, and make sure each one includes a main point. Use a topic sentence to introduce each paragraph.
5	Make sure you develop your points with details and evidence.
6	Remember, you are being assessed on your writing – you can include brief notes on illustrations and headings if appropriate, but do not waste time on drawing and layout. Use bullet points if the format requires it, but remember that you need to show you can write in complete sentences and paragraphs.
7	Many candidates lose marks because they are not careful with their grammar, punctuation, and sentence structures. Make sure you punctuate every sentence correctly, and use a mixture of simple, compound and complex sentences.
8	Check your punctuation – candidates often make mistakes in their use of commas, apostrophes and inverted commas. You will not achieve a pass at Level 2 if you cannot punctuate accurately.
9	Don't lose marks for spelling mistakes – check for common errors, and make sure you spell correctly any words that were included in the task.
10	Leave time to check your work carefully. Ask yourself: • Have I included everything I have been asked for? • Have I written enough? • Have I checked my work for spelling and punctuation mistakes?

Paper 2

(40 marks)

1 You have been working as a volunteer at the charity 'Animal Life'. You have been asked to give a speech at the mayor's fundraising dinner to persuade those present to offer their support.

You may wish to include some of the following information:

- Background on the Animal Life charity: it is a local charity looking after wild animals that have been injured, mostly by vehicles. Last year the charity saved 80% of the animals brought to them, and treated 357 animals in total.
- What the charity does.
- Why you are working there as a volunteer.
- How the charity is funded, and how much it costs to run.
- Why the charity needs support, and how much you are looking to raise.

Write the speech. [20]

2 You have received this letter from a friend:

> 4 Barnard St
> Peterlee
> County Durham
>
> Hi,
>
> How are you doing? I have been really busy with my studying and helping to sort out the paperwork for mum's move to Spain. How is your gran doing after her operation?
>
> The main reason I'm writing is to tell you about a charity parachute jump that I'm planning. I am not sure which charity to give the sponsor money to – what do you think? How do you think I will cope? Let me know – I've always valued your honest opinion! Will you sponsor me for the jump, as well?

Write a letter in response. [20]

Examiner tips

Read the questions

Always read the task carefully. Make notes on exactly what you are being asked to do. The examiner has made notes on Task 1 on the practice exam paper for you. Read them carefully.

Purpose: to persuade. Use persuasive techniques, e.g. emotive language, rhetorical questions, evidence to back up opinions, repetition of key words, anecdotes.

Audience: other people at the mayor's fundraising dinner. They need to know about the charity, and why it needs support.

Format: a speech. Use the key words in the list of ideas in the question as a structure for your speech.

Tone: it's an appeal for support in a formal situation: be polite, formal and persuasive.

ACTIVITY 1

Read Task 2 on the practice exam paper. Identify your purpose, audience, format and tone.

Plan carefully

Use your notes and the task to plan your work. Make sure you include everything you are asked for in the task.

ACTIVITY 2

Write a brief plan for a letter in response to Task 2 on the practice exam paper. Make sure you include all the relevant points in order, and aim to include one main point per paragraph.

Focus on accuracy

Always check your work for accuracy. Make sure your spelling, punctuation, and sentence structures are correct.

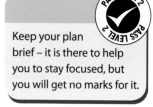

Keep your plan brief – it is there to help you to stay focused, but you will get no marks for it.

ACTIVITY 3

1 Complete the writing tasks. Remember your purpose, audience, format and tone for each, and use your notes and plans.
2 When you have finished, check your work for accuracy.

Study the answers below to question 1 on page 118. Use the examiner's comments to help you assess and improve your own writing skills.

Student A FAIL ✗

✗ Hiya,

My name's Lukas ✓ and I'm going to talk about why we want your money as we need your money to help save the lives of so many innocent animals. In our local area there are so many green areas and places where animals live, we have loads of animals that are really precious but these animals need your help. Loads of animals are hurt on the roads every year. ✗ I bet most of these are caused by young drivers who are driving too fast on the road. They just hit the animal and drive on. ✗ I think people who drive too fast on the roads should be banned for hurting animals and causing accidents.

✓ I've been working as a volunteer at an animal charity and I'm always shocked by how many animals are brought in to us and ✗ have been hit by cars. I think that people should support animal charities as the animals need our help and I hope that you can give us your support and money.

Comments:
- Tone – too informal.
- Clear introduction and correct format for a speech.
- Made up and vague.
- Not relevant.
- Accurate apostrophes.
- Repetition.

Examiner summary

The candidate begins with a clear introduction linked to the task. The correct format for a speech is used at first, but the writing becomes an unfocused narrative. The work is not always organised or divided into paragraphs, and the ideas are not sequenced or linked. Some of the text is vague, and there is little detail. The tone is often too informal and not persuasive. Because the candidate has not followed the bullet point suggestions in the task, he struggles for things to write and fails to meet his purpose. In the last sentence he finally makes an appeal for money, but there is little attempt to use persuasive techniques.

The spelling is accurate, but many of the words are repeated, and there are few examples of extended vocabulary. Full stops and commas are used accurately, but there is very little variety in the structure of sentences or punctuation. Sentences are of a similar length, and many begin with 'I'. Apostrophes are accurately used for contracted words.

This speech would not gain a pass at Level 2.

Student B PASS ✓

Good evening ladies and gentlemen, ✓

✓ My name is Maya and I am here to talk about a charity called Animal Life. Our charity was started by Linda Williams over 20 years ago to help animals that have been injured in the wild. The charity is run from Linda's farm house which she has converted into an animal hospital. ✓

Most of the animals that are treated at Animal Life have been injured by cars or other vehicles on the roads. Last year Animal Life managed to save over 80 per ✓ cent of the animals that were brought to them and treated over 357 ✓ injured or wounded animals. The charity gives these animals medication, operations, food and a place to live while they recover. Most of our animals are released back into the wild. We never turn animals away but sometimes there are just not enough volunteers or funds to give every animal the treatment it needs.

I have worked as a volunteer for over a year and spend four hours every Saturday working at the farm. I've had fun helping with the animals and it's really good to watch them get better and be put back in the wild.

The charity costs over £300, 000 to run each year and we are looking for extra sponsorship from local businesses that can support our fundraising. We hope to build a new barn and duck pond next year so your help would be really appreciated. We are looking to raise an extra £150,000 to help build our new projects.

✓ Please help. Wild animals don't have owners and without us there would be no one to help them. We save as many animals as we can but with your help we could save more. Thank you. ✓

Correct format and tone.

Clear introduction.

Follows the bullet points in the task.

Use of figures/ evidence is effective.

Correct format and tone.

Some persuasive writing.

Examiner summary

This is a focused and clear speech that includes the information set out in the task. From the formal opening, there is a clear understanding of the format, purpose and audience for this task, and the candidate maintains the formal tone throughout. The work is well sequenced, and organised into clear paragraphs giving the details suggested in some of the bullet points. The speech uses a range of vocabulary and some basic persuasive techniques, although these are mostly used only in the last few sentences.

The writing has been well punctuated and includes a range of different sentence structures. The candidate uses full stops and some commas correctly, and the grammar is secure. Spelling is accurate.

This is a secure Level 2 piece of writing.

Study the answers below to question 2 on page 118. Use the examiner's comments to help you assess and improve your own writing skills.

Student A FAIL ✗

Emma Jones
London
12th June

Sender's name not needed here. Incomplete address.

✗ Alright Mazie,

Slang.

✗ Doin good and glad you are too. Got a new boyfriend and he is lush, we have been going out for about six months now and all the family like him a lot even gran. Talkin ✗ of gran, her hip op went well and she is now back home with Uncle Ted where she is going to stay until she is better, even granddad thinks this is a good idea but we all think he is enjoying the piece ✗ and quite as you know how much gran likes to talk. How is your mums ✗ move to Spain going I thought she was meant to go last month, we would all luv to go out and stay in that huge house she showed us on the emil, ✗ is that the one she is really going to buy? ✗

I had to read the letter twice when you said you was ✗ going to do a parashoot ✗ jump and even my mum thought you had gone mad. You don't even like clibmin up to the top of two flights of stairs in our house, never mind jumpin out of a plane. I think it is a good idea to do somethin for charity and ✓ you could always do it for the breast cancer charity as that would make your mum really proud of you knowin what her mum went through but you probably need to think of a better way of raising the cash than this stupid idea

Many spelling errors.

Missing apostrophe.

Background can be included, but too much material is not relevant.

Incorrect grammar.

Some link to the task here.

No closure.

Long, unstructured sentences and comma splices.

Spelling error could have been avoided by checking the task wording.

Examiner summary

Informal letters need to include the sender's address. Make sure it is correctly presented. This address is not complete and the writer's name should never appear here. The contents of the letter are detailed and the candidate has tried to establish a relationship with 'Mazie' by answering her questions and including personal details. This works quite well in places, but too much time is spent on this material, which is not asked for in the task. There is a clear awareness of the purpose and task, and an understanding of the audience. The tone is correctly informal. Vocabulary is suited to the task, but is too limited.

The candidate uses slang: this is never acceptable in an examination, even for informal writing. There are many basic spelling and grammar errors. Many of the sentences are too long and lack correct punctuation. Comma splices are a problem throughout.

This letter would not gain a pass at Level 2.

Student B PASS ✓

Correct address layout.

✓ 4 Newbridge Road
Ightham
Kent

Hi Sara,

✓ Thanks for your letter. It felt like ages since we had written to each other and it was good to hear all of the news. I bet your mum really appreciates you helping her out with her paperwork and I hope that the planned move to Spain is going well. Gran is doing well after her operation and has just come out of hospital.

✓ Right, on to the main point of your letter, the parachute jump. I think it is a really good idea for you to have something to work towards and a parachute jump will be something a bit different for you. It's really good that you are jumping for charity. I thought you might think about doing it for Age Concern. Now that Gran is getting on a bit, she has had some help from the local Age Concern volunteers who visited her in hospital and have been round to visit since she got home.

✓ I think you will be fine, but you do need to make sure you are well prepared and more importantly find yourself a fit instructor ✓ – no point in jumping out of an aeroplane unless it's with a fit bloke! ✓ Honestly, as long as you know what you are doing and you listen carefully to the instructor, then I think you will be fine. Take care and let me know how we can sponsor you.

Love, Jamila

Appropriate amount of background material.

Clear focus on the task.

Informal tone with use of some humour is appropriate for the task.

Punctuation is correct, and varied in places.

Correct closure.

Examiner summary

Although this response is rather brief, the writing is sensibly sequenced and the candidate includes some of their own ideas and comments to make the letter sound realistic. Paragraphs are used to structure the writing, and make the separate ideas clear for the reader. The candidate uses humour in the final section to further engage readers. Ideas are relatively simple and not always expanded, but overall the letter is clear and focused on the task. Vocabulary is relatively simple, too, but suits the tone and audience of the writing, although 'really' is overused.

Spelling is accurate, including extended vocabulary. Punctuation is accurate, and there are some varied sentence structures and lengths adding variety to the writing. The candidate uses a variety of punctuation to add to the lively and friendly tone.

A natural, focused and accurate piece of writing, which would be awarded a pass at Level 2.

Progress checker

Check your progress

Review your work using the following steps to get a rounded picture of how well you have done and what you need to do to improve.

1 Look at the notes that were given alongside the texts, on pages 103, 107, 112–14 and 116–17. Read what the examiner had to say about the tasks and the annotated questions. Check to see if you have covered everything in your own answers.

2 Check your work against the example student answers, on pages 108–11, 113–14 and 120–23. Which answer is yours most similar to? Are there areas you have missed? Did you think of any additional ideas? Read the examiner's comments for extra advice that will help you improve your own work. Did you make any of the same mistakes as the 'fail' student? Did you achieve any of the same points as the 'pass' student?

3 On pages 125–7 the examiner has included a number of key features that you should have included in your answers for each of the assessment questions. Go through each task in turn and check your own work against the list to see which of these features you have included and which are missing.

4 Once you have completed steps 1–3, work out if you are within or below Level 2. Use the following indicators to rate your own answers.

High Level 2	Secure Level 2	Below Level 2
You have included all of the points that the examiner suggested, most of the ideas from the progress checkers and perhaps a few of your own. It is likely that you are working at a high Level 2.	You have included most of the points that the examiner suggested and most of the ideas from the progress checkers. It is likely that you are working at a secure Level 2.	You have struggled to answer a question or complete a task and there are a number of areas that you did not include in your answer. You are working below a Level 2 for that task.

5 Write an action plan. To help you, look back at the examiner's comments for ideas. Their notes for the 'fail' student give clear guidance on what the student needs to do to improve their response. Those for the 'pass' student state what they have done to earn a pass. Which three points relate most closely to your own work? Is there anything else you think you should work on? For example, in the Reading examination:

My reading answers missed out some important points. Next time I should:
- make sure I check how many marks are available for each question and include enough points to achieve them
- make sure I start at the top of the text and work through so that I don't miss anything out
- keep an eye on my timings to make sure I allow enough time for each question.

Check your progress in Reading

For all questions, did you:

- check how many marks the question was worth
- use the right text or texts?

Question 1 tested your ability to read and summarise information from a single source. Did you:

- use your scanning skills to look for the key word 'symptoms'
- highlight ten different symptoms
- summarise the highlighted points in your own words in a clear paragraph?

Question 2 tested your ability to detect implicit meaning and understand how meaning is conveyed. Did you:

- make sure that for every point you made you explained how and why it helps teenagers
- comment on the clear, self-explanatory title
- comment on the picture that helps teenagers realise depression can happen to anyone
- comment on the use of questions that work like a checklist to help teenagers decide if they may be depressed
- comment on the direct tone used in the introduction so that the issue of depression is not ignored
- comment on the clear bullet point list of symptoms
- comment on the use of questions as headings that help the reader to find the answers
- comment on the range of treatments available
- use evidence from the text in your answer?

Question 3 tested your ability to select and utilise different information. Did you:

- locate the key words 'treat' and 'GP'/'doctor' in each text
- locate the correct area of each text and highlight different treatments
- write down a range of different treatments?

Question 4 tested your ability to select and utilise different information. Did you:

- realise that the key word 'caused' suggests the information might be at the start of the text
- close read the text looking for causes and include a range in your answer
- realise that the word 'What' means that you only have to find the causes – not explain them?

Question 5 tested your ability to identify the purpose of a text and comment on how meaning is conveyed. Did you:

- re-scan the text to understand why it had been written (the purpose)
- start your answer by giving at least one of these purposes: to give information, to give advice, to share his experience or to help other people
- use evidence to back up your ideas?

Question 6 tested your ability to analyse and use texts based on the needs of the audience. Did you:

- set out your answer appropriately as advice for a friend
- highlight in the three texts the points you could include
- make sure you did not repeat anything?

Check your progress in Speaking, listening and communication

Task 2 tested your ability to plan and give a presentation.

Did you plan:

- to suit your audience (the police)
- a brief introduction to explain who you are, and a note of where and when the accident took place
- to 'set the scene' with information on weather, other people, clues that might suggest an accident
- a description of what actually happened
- to note who was involved and any witnesses, including their behaviour, reactions and injuries
- to state what happened in the time after the crash
- a brief summary to explain why it happened?

If you gave your presentation, did you

- use language appropriate for a formal presentation to the police
- include all the points in your plan
- clearly sequence and organise your ideas
- present your ideas carefully and clearly so the police could fully understand exactly what happened
- use enough detail and expand your ideas, where necessary
- answer any questions in detail – not just a brief answer?

Task 3 tested your ability to plan for and take part in a discussion.

Did you plan:

- with the audience of your discussion in mind
- whether you were for or against the proposal
- a brief introduction to explain who you are and why you feel it is important to join the discussion
- an explanation of your point of view
- a list of reasons for or against the curfew
- an explanation of how it could affect you, your family or your business
- possible alternative solutions
- a summary of your main points
- how to answer any likely questions?

If you took part in the discussion, did you:

- use language appropriate to the formal situation
- include the ideas in your plan in a clearly sequenced and well-organised way
- adapt your ideas to suit the other members of the discussion group
- encourage others in the discussion to support your views
- use enough detail and expand your ideas, where necessary
- answer any questions in detail – not just a brief answer
- ask sensible questions of other members of the discussion group
- help the discussion to move forward?

Check your progress in Writing

All writing answers are marked for:

- content and organisation – the quality of the information you include and the way you set out your work
- sentence structure, punctuation, and spelling – the accuracy and variety of your sentences and punctuation, and your ability to spell correctly.

Content and organisation

For both questions, did you:

- stay aware of the purpose and layout of the task
- write with the audience in mind, and include words and phrases to appeal to them
- plan carefully to include a wide range of ideas
- give realistic reasons to support your opinions and ideas, where necessary
- sequence your ideas to be clear and have an impact on the reader
- use paragraphs to structure your ideas
- include a wide range of vocabulary to influence the reader's response to your work?

Sentence structure, punctuation and spelling

For both questions, did you:

- vary the subjects of sentences (e.g. avoid overusing 'I')
- vary the lengths of sentences
- use simple, compound and complex sentences
- confidently use a wide range of punctuation to structure sentences
- spell words correctly
- use correct grammar, including tenses and subject-verb agreement?

Heinemann is an imprint of Pearson Education Limited, a company incorporated in England and Wales, having its registered office at Edinburgh Gate, Harlow, Essex, CM20 2JE. Registered company number: 872828

www.pearsonschoolsandfecolleges.co.uk

Heinemann is a registered trademark of Pearson Education Limited

Text © Pearson Education Limited 2010

First published 2010

12 11 10 09 08
10 9 8 7 6 5 4 3 2 1

British Library Cataloguing in Publication Data
A catalogue record for this book is available from the British Library.

ISBN 978 0 435 01681 4

Designed and produced by Kamae Design, Oxford
Original illustrations © Pearson Education Limited 2010
Illustrated by Ian Lansley p.24
Cover design by Wooden Ark Studios
Picture research by Virginia Stroud-Lewis
Cover photo © Masterfile
Printed by Rotolito in Italy

Acknowledgements
The authors and publisher would like to thank the following individuals and organisations for permission to reproduce photographs:

p.5 Alamy/Bill Bachmann; p.6 Ron Hilton/iStockphoto; p.7 Getty Images/Tim Graham; p.9 Joe Gough/Shutterstock; p.11 Bubbles; p.13 Alamy/Darryl Webb; p.15 Ricardo Moraes/AP/Press Association Images; p.16 dragon_fang/Shutterstock; p.18 Getty Images/Oli Scarff; p.21 iStockphoto/phildate; p.23 BlueOrange Studio/Shutterstock; p.25 (top) Getty Images/Lilly Dong; p.25 (bottom) Getty Images/WireImage/Tomos Brangwyn; p.29 Getty Images/SimplyMui Photography; p.31 Alamy/The Photolibrary Wales/Billy Stock; p.33 (top) Corbis/Philippe Lissac/Godong; p.33 (bottom) Alamy/epf model; p.41 Alamy/Dennis MacDonald; p.42 Alamy/Angela Hampton Picture Library; p.43 Corbis/Martyn Goddard; p.44 Jeff Morgan industry and work/Alamy; p.47 Getty Images/Stone/Rene Sheret; pp.48/49 Alamy/Janine Wiedel Photolibrary; p.53 Dean Mitchell/Shutterstock; p.54 Alamy/Ian Shaw; p.55 Getty Images/Photographer's Choice/Tim Hawley; p.56 Monika Wisniewskai/Stockphoto; p.62 Sally and Richard Greenhill/Alamy; p.71 Ed Hidden/iStockphoto; pp.72/73 Alamy/Picture Partners; p.78 Getty Images/Photographer's Choice/Peter Dazeley; p.80 Alamy/David Askham; p.87 Monkey Business Images/Shutterstock; p.88 David Cumming; Eye Ubiquitous/Corbis; p.94 Alamy/Paul Doyle; p.95 Getty Images/Photographer's Choice/Peter Dazeley; p.96 Rainer Jensen/epa/Corbis; p.104 Corbis/Tomas Rodriguez.

The publisher would like to thank the following for permission to reproduce copyright material:

pp.5, 41, 53 QCA Functional English Standards reproduced by permission of QCA (Enterprises) Limited; p.6 "What drugs do to you" extract from http://www.nhs.uk/Livewell/drugs/Pages/Drugsoverview.aspx reproduced by permission of NHS Choices; p.7 extract from "Drug taking and driving" from www.nya.org.uk reproduced by permission of the National Youth Agency/www.nya.org.uk; p.9 extract from "Britain: the nation that can't even boil an egg" by Jo Willey, Daily Express 29/8/2007 reproduced by permission of the Daily Express and Northern and Shell Media Publications; p.11 'Schools buying stronger chairs as pupils get bigger' by Laura Clark, Daily Mail 2/4/2009 reproduced by permission of Solo Syndication; p.13 extract from http://www.direct.gov.uk/en/YoungPeople/CrimeAndJustice/KeepingSafe/DG_10027660 reproduced by permission of Crown Copyright; p.14 extract from "Please free them, begs mother of Rio holiday 'fraudster'" by Rebecca Camber, Daily Mail 30/07/2009 reproduced by permission of Solo Syndication; p.15 "Why should anyone feel sorry for these spoilt stupid girls" by Bryony Gordon, Daily Telegraph 22/8/2009 reproduced by permission of Telegraph Media Group Limited 2009; p.17 extract from Real life identity theft – Mr A from www.stop-idfraud.ie/real-life-stories.php#mra reproduced by permission of Fellowes Ltd; p.17 abridged text from http://www.checkmyfile.com/articles/43/identity-theft/identity-thieves-target-myspace-and-facebook.htm reproduced by permission of checkmyfile; p.19 knife crime poster reproduced by permission of Crimestoppers UK; p.21 extract from "A mobile, the gizmo we just can't live without" by Sophie Borland, Daily Mail 1/8/2008 reproduced by permission of Solo Syndication; p.25 "Travel Safe" leaflet reproduced by permission of the British Transport Police; p.25 extract from "The World according to Jeremy Clarkson" by Jeremy Clarkson, (Michael Joseph, 2004) reproduced by permission of the Penguin Group; p.27 extract from "10 Top reasons to stay smokefree" reproduced by permission of GASP www.gasp.org.uk; p.29 amended text from www.deafnessresearch.org.uk reproduced by permission of Deafness Research UK; p.43 extract from "Spy-under-the-bonnet sneaks to mum and dad when young drivers take risks on the road" by Ben Webster, The Times, 28/2/2009 reproduced by permission of NI Syndication on behalf of The Times; p.47 Extract from "A Guide to Uni Life" by Lucy Tobin reproduced with permission of Trotman Publishing, an imprint of Crimson Publishing Ltd © Trotman Publishing, 2009; p.49 edited extract from www.the-mosquito.com/the-mosquito.htm reproduced by permission of Compound Security; p.49 abridged text from "What is a Mosquito" from www.liberty-human-rights.org.uk reproduced by permission of Liberty and Civil Liberties Trust; p.87 leaflet reproduced by permission of Great Ormond Street Hospital Children's Charity © gosh.org; p.104 extract from www.teenissues.co.uk/Teenage-Depression.html reproduced by permission of PtS and TeenIssues..

Every effort has been made to contact copyright holders of material reproduced in this book. Any omissions will be rectified in subsequent printings if notice is given to the publishers.

Websites
There are links to relevant websites in this book. In order to ensure that the links are up to date, that the links work, and that the sites are not inadvertently linked to sites that could be considered offensive, we have made the links available on the Pearson website at www.pearsonhotlinks.co.uk. When you access the site, the express code is 6814P.